Treasures from the Original Vol. II:

Studies in Philippians

DR. HAROLD J. BERRY

Originally published as *Gems from the Original Vol. III: Studies in Philippians.*

Gems from the Original Vol. III was published by The Good News Broadcasting Association, Inc. © 1978.

Unless otherwise identified, all Scripture quotations in this publication are taken from the *New American Standard Bible*, © 1960, 1962, 1963, 1968, 1971, 1972, 1973, 1975, 1977, 1995 by the Lockman Foundation and are used by permission.

Loved (5.5x8.5) Self-Publishing Template © 2017 Renee Fisher [https://www.reneefisher.com]

Cover Design: © Nelly Murariu at PixBeeDesign.com

ISBN-10: 0-578-63722-7
ISBN-13: 978-0-578-63722-8

Dedication

To my wife, Donna M. Berry, who passed away on October 13, 2019. We had both trusted Jesus as Savior when we were young. We met in Bible College after she had her RN. She also had four years of Bible College. We were married 65 years telling others about Jesus and how to be ready for eternity. When it came her time to pass away she was at complete peace about meeting Jesus face to face. She was a godly wife, mother and grandmother.

Contents

Foreword

HOW MANY OF US, when we don't understand something complex says, "It's all Greek to me?" My good friend, Harold Berry, has made New Testament Greek understandable for which I am very grateful. In his Book on Philippians, Harold has translated Greek to allow us to gain insight and understanding of these letters to the New Testament churches.

Harold and I have known each other for well over thirty years, and have served together on Back to the Bible Board of Trustees during that time. Harold served as Chair and I was privileged to serve with him as Vice Chair until he chose to step back, but remain on the Board and asked me to become Chair. His experience, theological insight, and knowledge of the Word have been a great addition to our ability to serve God and this ministry. I highly recommend your use of this book as a great reference to help you understand the original text of the New Testament.

With Great Respect,

Dale E. Michels, MD.
Board Chair
Back to the Bible

Chapter 1 – To the Saints in Christ at Philippi

Paul and Timothy, bond-servants of Christ Jesus, to all the saints in Christ Jesus who are in Philippi, including the overseers and deacons (1:1).

IN ACCORDANCE WITH the first-century custom, the writer of this letter began with his own name—Paul. He was also known by the name "Saul," as is evident from the Book of the Acts. However, in his New Testament epistles, he is prominently known as Paul. Sometimes interpreters maintain that at the time of his conversion he adopted the Gentile name "Paul" in place of his Hebrew name "Saul." It is more likely, however, that Paul bore both names from his early years, as was customary of the times. After conversion he probably used his Gentile name (Paul) most of the time to more closely identify himself as an apostle to the Gentiles (see Gal. 2:7-8).

Paul customarily mentioned his apostleship in the opening remarks of his New Testament letters. However, in writing to the Philippians he did not allude to his apostleship. This is an indication of how intensely personal this letter was to the believers in Philippi who had become his close friends. His authority and apostleship were unquestioned, so there was no need to specify himself as an apostle.

Paul also mentioned his co-worker Timothy. Timothy, as well as Paul, was well known to the believers in Philippi, as will be noted later concerning the background of the church at

Philippi.

Paul described himself and Timothy as "bond-servants of Christ." There is no definite article (the) in the Greek text. The construction is as if a colon were placed after Timothy, which would cause the phrase to read "Paul and Timothy: bond-servants of Christ Jesus."

The word translated "bond-servants" was well known throughout the Roman Empire with its system of slavery. The word is *doulos*, which means "slave" or "bound one." "Servant" is an acceptable translation if one realizes the strong meaning of the word. All believers, including Paul and Timothy, are owned by their Master, for they have been "bought with a price" (1 Cor. 6:20). Paul viewed the believer as a slave to sin who had been bought out of the marketplace and set free by Jesus Christ. Because a believer is set free from the bondage of sin, he willingly makes himself a slave to Jesus Christ.

"Bond-Servants of Christ Jesus" was the only reference Paul needed to make concerning himself and Timothy as he wrote to the Philippians. This implied all that was necessary concerning their relationship to their Lord and Savior.

Paul then specified the recipients of his letter: "To all the saints in Christ Jesus who are in Philippi." Paul referred to his readers as "saints." The Greek word used is *hagios* and is related to other words translated by a form of "holy" or "sanctified." The Greek words do not refer to a state of sinless perfection but to being set apart for God. The one who trusts Jesus Christ as personal Savior is at that moment set apart to God.

Positionally, a believer has a perfect sanctification in God; but experientially, the believer retains a sin nature and needs to be more and more set apart in his daily walk as he matures in the Lord. The Philippian believers were set apart in Jesus

Christ, but they were by no means perfect.

As to their spiritual location, they were "in Christ Jesus"; as to their geographical location, they were "in Philippi."

The words "in Christ" or "in Christ Jesus" are distinctively characteristic of Church-age believers. These terms are never used of Old Testament believers or of believers after the Church Age, such as during the Tribulation. That believers are in Christ is indicated in 1 Corinthians 12:13: "For by one Spirit we were all baptized into one body, whether Jews or Greeks, whether slaves or free, and we were all made to drink of one Spirit."

The "one body" referred to is the Body of Christ. This is evident from Ephesians 1:22-23: "And He put all things in subjection under His feet, and gave Him as head over all things to the church, which is His body, the fullness of Him who fills all in all."

These verses show that the Heavenly Father has put all things under the authority of Jesus Christ, who is the head of the Church. Every believer—from the Day of Pentecost (Acts 2) to the Rapture, or the translation of the Church at the end of the Church Age (1 Cor. 15:51-52; 1 Thess. 4:16-17)—is a member of the body of Christ and, therefore, is in Christ. This group is commonly referred to as the "universal Church," for it is composed of all those around the world who have received Jesus Christ as Savior.

The words "in Philippi" reveal the geographical location of the believers to whom Paul was writing. When believers meet together in a given locality, they are commonly referred to as a "local church." The city of Philippi, about 800 miles from Rome, was founded in the fourth century B.C. by Philip II, the Father of Alexander the Great.

Paul had visited Philippi on various occasions, but the most significant time was when he first visited the city, as recorded in the Book of the Acts. Paul was on his second missionary journey at the time, having started in Jerusalem accompanied by Silas (15:36-41). When they came to Derbe and Lystra, Timothy joined them and was with Paul and Silas when Paul received a vision from the Lord to go to Macedonia (16:1-11). Arriving at Philippi, the most important city in that part of Macedonia and a colony of the Roman Empire, they preached the gospel to those who gathered at a riverside (vv. 12-13).

At Philippi a woman named Lydia trusted Christ as Savior and provided hospitality for Paul and his companions. It was here that Paul had rebuked an evil spirit in a girl being used to bring her masters profit. As a result, he and Silas were brought before the magistrates of the city, beaten and thrown into prison.

Later, when Paul and Silas were delivered from prison by a miracle of God, the rulers of the city were horrified to learn that Paul and Silas were Roman citizens (v. 38). One of the rights of a Roman citizen was freedom from scourging, and the magistrates realized that they might be in trouble with the imperial government for what they had done. Paul was in no hurry to leave the city, and it was only after he had visited with the believers that he finally left (v. 40). The believers at Philippi followed Paul's ministry with interest and even sent contributions to further his work (Phil. 4:15-16).

As Paul wrote his Philippian letter, he was in prison in Rome; thus, it is referred to as one of the "prison epistles" along with Ephesians, Colossians and Philemon. This was an earlier imprisonment than the one during which he wrote his last letter, 2 Timothy.

In addressing those at Philippi, Paul added: "including the overseers and deacons." The word "overseers" is a translation of the plural form of *episkopos*. It is commonly considered that this word refers to the same position as *presbuteros*, meaning "elder." "Overseer" (*episkopos*) refers to what the person does, whereas "elder" (*presbuteros*) refers to the position itself. Paul's reference was to the ruling body in the local church. Qualifications for this office are listed in 1 Timothy 3:1-7.

"Deacons" is the plural form of *diakonos*, meaning "servant." The basis of such a position in the local church is supplied by Acts 6:1-7. It became necessary to take care of the physical needs among the believers. Rather than have the apostles leave the study of the Word and their ministry of prayer, men were chosen to "serve (*diakoneō*) tables (v. 2). The Greek word translated "serve" in this verse is the verb form of the word translated "deacons" in Philippians 1:1. The qualifications for the office of deacon are listed in I Timothy 3:8-13. Whereas the overseers, or elders, are responsible for the ministry of the Word and the spiritual needs of a local church, deacons are responsible for the physical or material needs of a local church.

Grace to you and peace from God our Father and the Lord Jesus Christ (1:2).

"Grace" was a word of greeting, but it was a key word in Paul's vocabulary. He never ceased to be amazed at God's salvation by grace through faith in Christ alone. Paul realized he deserved condemnation, and he marveled that God loved him enough to send His Son to die in his place. The word "grace" emphasizes God's unmerited favor to mankind. Salvation is of grace; it cannot be earned, only received (see Eph. 2:8-9).

The result of responding to the grace of God is peace. Peace with God is acquired at the time of salvation. Paul said, "Therefore, having been justified by faith, we have peace with God through our Lord Jesus Christ" (Rom. 5:1). But not all who have peace *with* God have the peace *of* God. Paul urges believers: "Be anxious for nothing, but in everything by prayer and supplication with thanksgiving let your requests be made known to God. And the peace of God, which surpasses all comprehension, will guard your hearts and your minds in Christ Jesus" (Phil. 4:6-7).

Paul emphasized the origin of grace and peace when he wrote the Philippians: "From God our Father and from the Lord Jesus Christ." Although the third Person of the Trinity, the Holy Spirit, is not mentioned in this verse, it is evident from other passages that the Spirit's ministry is to take what originates with the Father and the Son and apply it to the believer's life.

Jesus Christ said of the Holy Spirit, "He will glorify Me, for He will take of Mine and will disclose *it* to you" (John 16:14). Grace and peace are particularly viewed as originating with the Father and the Son inasmuch as the Father sent the Son to be the Savior of the world. Salvation was possible only by the Son's giving His life and becoming the propitiation for our sins (see John 3:16, 1 John 2:2). No wonder Paul's heart was filled with gratitude toward the Father and the Son as he wrote to believers in Jesus Christ.

Chapter 2 – Pleasant Memories and Prayers

I thank my God in all my remembrance of you (1:3).

IN THIS VERSE we see how grateful Paul was for the believers in Philippi. It had been about 10 years since he had first visited them, and yet every memory of them brought a sense of gratitude to him.

With Paul, it wasn't just a matter of occasionally thanking God as he remembered the Philippians. The word translated "I thank" is *eucharisteō*, and the tense here emphasizes continual action, or practice. The word itself is related to the Greek words for grace (*charis*) and joy (*chara*). Although several years had passed since Paul had last visited Philippi, he had vivid memories of the believers there, and it was his practice to thank God for them as he remembered them.

Paul would also have had memories of his first visit to Philippi that were not so pleasant. He would have remembered the imprisonment and beating that he and Silas suffered. But he would also have recalled God's act in delivering them from prison, which resulted in the salvation of the jailer and his family (see Acts 16:22-34).

Notice how Paul referred to God when he said, "I thank my God" (1:3) Here we see the personal element in Paul's relationship with God. Christianity was more to Paul than a body of facts to be defended; it was a personal relationship with a Person. Here we see the warmth of his heart in response to the God he served. Because of this vital relationship with God, Paul was motivated to take the gospel to others—such as the Philippians—even though there was risk of punishment and even loss of life.

Paul told the Philippians he thanked his God "in all my remembrance of you." Upon or "in" (epi) reveals the basis of his thanks—"all my remembrance of you." As far as the Philippian believers were concerned, Paul had no memory that did not bring a response of thanks from his heart to God. Seeing these people accept Jesus Christ as personal Savior more than compensated for what Paul had endured to get the gospel to them. Surely there would have been times when they, as new Christians, would have done unwise things, since they were not mature believers in the early years. But even memories of this type brought joy to Paul's heart as he thought about them and their zeal for the Lord.

Always offering prayer with joy in my every prayer for you all (1:4).

Observe Paul's use of inclusive terms in this verse— always, every, all. Each is related to the same Greek word, translated "every" in verse 3. By using these inclusive terms in verse 4, Paul stressed that with every memory of the Philippian believers he always made request with joy. And he did not exclude any of them from his prayers. This fact is emphasized by the words "you all."

Inasmuch as Greek has a plural form of "you," Paul would not have needed to use the word "all" to reveal that he was praying for the entire group. But by using the word "all" he emphasized his inclusion of every Philippian believer in his prayers.

It is apparent from this verse that Paul did not just pray, "Bless the Philippian believers." Even the word translated "prayer" emphasizes a particular petition for some gift. Paul was aware of individual needs, and he prayed in a personal way for every Philippian believer.

However, Paul's prayers were more than just a listing of needs that he knew the Philippians had, for there was a jubilant attitude in his praying—"offering prayer with joy." Paul considered it a privilege to pray for the believers in Philippi, for it brought joy to him just to pray for them. The word translated "offering" is in a tense that also emphasizes Paul's constant practice of making requests with joy for them.

"Remembrance" in verse 3 and "offering prayer with joy" in verse 4 are directly related to verse 5.

In view of your participation in the gospel from the first day until now (1:5).

"For" is from the same Greek word (*epi*) that is translated "upon" or "in" in verse 3. Here also it shows the basis for Paul's thankfulness in making request with joy.

Paul's word for "participation" is the same word for the word "fellowship," which was a common first-century word—*koinonia*. But he lifted the word to a new height as he spoke of fellowship "in the gospel."

The fellowship involved seemed to have been more than just believers coming together to share from their lives with one another. Although this would be included, the word "in" indicates more. It is a translation of *eis*, which is commonly translated "unto." It has the sense of "with a view to" or, in this case, "with the gospel in view." Certainly, it would include a sharing of all that Jesus Christ meant to them, but the fellowship in evangelizing the lost seems to be the element uppermost in Paul's mind. It was a fellowship with the gospel in view—the good news that Jesus Christ has paid the penalty for sin so that anyone can be delivered from condemnation by receiving Him as Savior.

Paul remembered and gave thanks for their fellowship in the gospel "from the first day until now." "The first day" refers to that time when Paul first came to Philippi to present the gospel. From the time that the recipients of his letter responded to Jesus Christ, they had been fellowshipping with each other and laboring together to take the gospel to others. From that time to the time of Paul's writing, the Philippian believers had been a source of joy to him. They had been deeply etched in his memory, as indicated by his practice of praying for them and making requests for them with joy.

Chapter 3 –
Philippians' Mutual
Love, Partnership

For I am **confident of this very thing, that He who began a good work in you will perfect it until the day of Christ Jesus (1:6).**

THE WORDS "BEING CONFIDENT" are translated from a Greek word that occurs in the perfect tense. This tense emphasizes an act completed in the past with a continuing effect. At the time of Paul's writing, he had been and still was confident of what he said in verse 6. His confidence had been established in the past, and it continued right up to the present.

Notice what Paul was confident of: "That He who began a good work in you will perfect it until the day of Christ Jesus." Paul was referring to God, who began His work in the Philippians as evidenced by their salvation about 10 years earlier. This good work not only included salvation but also what God was doing in their lives at the time Paul wrote to them. The context indicates that Paul was also referring to the bonds of fellowship that he had with the Philippians. The Philippian believers had cooperated with Paul and had a deep affection for him; thus, Paul had been—and still was—convinced that what God had begun in them in this regard would continue.

It is significant that Paul used the words "in you." Although God works through individuals to accomplish His will, His primary work is in the believer as He changes his attitudes and motives into those that please Him.

The Word translated "perfect" is *epiteleō*, meaning, "end, finish, complete." The entire work was of God—He began it, and He would complete it. What a marvelous thing it is to see lives revolutionized by God as individuals trust Jesus Christ as Savior. Those who previously sought fellowship with others in sin have their desires and motivations so changed that they aggressively seek out fellowship with those who are also believers. No wonder Paul said, "Therefore if anyone is in Christ, he is a new creature; the old things passed away; behold, new things have come" (2 Corinthians 5:17).

Notice how long Paul expected God to keep working in the believers—"until the day of Christ Jesus." Paul did not know when believers might be caught up to meet the Lord in the air, but he knew that God's work in the Philippian believers would continue until that time.

For it is only right for me to feel this way about you all, because I have you in my heart, since both in my imprisonment and in the defense and confirmation of the gospel, you all are partakers of grace with me (1:7).

The word translated "right" is *dikaios*, meaning "right" or "just" and is often translated "righteous." The context indicates the meaning here is "right" or "just." It was right for Paul to think this way about the Philippian believers—it would have been wrong for him not to think as he did concerning them. Also, the word Paul used for "feel" meant more than just to have a thought or to suppose something; it was more of an attitude, having a certain mind-set. Paul had an attitude of confidence concerning the Philippian believers, and this confidence accompanied the petitions he made for them.

The reason it was right for Paul to have this attitude toward the Philippians is seen in the statement "because I have you in my heart." The word translated "heart" is *kardia*. Although it is common in 21st-century English usage to think of the heart as the seat of the emotions, this was not the case in Greek usage. The heart was viewed as the center of intellect, sensibility (emotions) and will, with as much or more emphasis on intellect and will as on emotions. The seat of the emotions was referred to by another word, which occurs in verse 8 and will be discussed at that point.

Paul had the Philippians in his heart in that they were in his mind and will, for he thought about them often and prayed specifically for them.

The reason they had found such a place in Paul's heart is seen in his words: "Since both in my imprisonment and in the defense and confirmation of the gospel, you all are partakers of grace with me." Because of the reference to "imprisonment" and "defense" some think that Paul was referring to a specific trial he was undergoing before the Imperial Court. Others, however, think these terms were used in a more general sense and refer to all of the hardships Paul suffered and to the defenses he had made for the gospel.

As to Paul's hardships, he wrote elsewhere: "Five times I received from the Jews thirty-nine *lashes*. Three times I was beaten with rods, once I was stoned, three times I was shipwrecked, a night and a day I have spent in the deep. *I have been* on frequent journeys, in dangers from rivers, dangers from robbers, dangers from *my* countrymen, danger from the Gentiles, dangers in the city, dangers in the wilderness, dangers on the sea, dangers among false brethren; *I have been* in labor and hardship, through many sleepless nights, in hunger and thirst, often without food, in cold and exposure. Apart from *such* external things, there is the daily pressure on me of concern for all the churches. Who is weak without my being weak? Who is led into sin without my intense concern?" (2 Cor. 11:24-29).

Indications are that the Philippian believers had carefully followed Paul's ministry, had faithfully prayed for him and had contributed to his financial needs. Thus, his bonds were considered to be their bonds. His defense of the gospel was considered to be their defense of the gospel. They seemed to have experienced what is said in 1 Corinthians 12:26: "And if *one* member suffers, all the members suffer with it; if one member is honored, all the members rejoice with it."

The word translated "defense" is *apologia*, from which the word "apologetics" is derived. This same Greek word also appears in Philippians 1:16. And it occurs in 2 Timothy 4:16, where Paul was specifically referring to his trial before the Imperial Court.

Paul referred to the "confirmation of the gospel" (Phil. 1:7). The word Paul used (*bebaioō*) means "to confirm" in the sense of establishing. In setting forth his case for the gospel, Paul was actually establishing the validity of the gospel wherever he went. Notice the defense and confirmation were not of himself but of the gospel. Although Paul and the gospel could not be separated, it was always Paul's intent to focus attention on the gospel, not on himself. The "gospel" (*euaggelion*) literally means "good news." This Good News was that Jesus had died on the cross and paid the penalty for sin so that anyone might have eternal life by receiving Him as Savior.

Concerning Paul's imprisonment and his defense and confirmation of the gospel, he told the Philippians, "You all are partakers of grace with me." They were participants with him in the enabling grace he had received from God to bear up under the bonds of suffering and to give an effective defense of the gospel. Paul did not consider the Philippians as mere spectators of what he was doing but as actual participants with him as he sought to glorify the Lord and to evangelize the lost.

For God is my witness, how I long for you all with the affection of Christ Jesus (1:8).

Here Paul expresses his emotions toward the Philippian believers. Inasmuch as one person cannot look inside another person to see his emotions, Paul said, "God is my witness." He was emphasizing that God knew how affectionately he thought of the Philippian believers, even though they could not see the seat of his emotions. Paul longed for the Philippians, and this longing was more than his own desires; it was "in the affection of Christ Jesus."

The word translated "affection" is *splagchnon* and is the word used to refer to the seat of the emotions. As mentioned in connection with verse 7, "heart" was not used to refer to the seat of the emotions; *splagchnon* was reserved for this purpose. This word literally meant "inward parts" or "entrails" and is used in that way in Acts 1:18. However, the figurative use refers to the seat of emotions such as love and affection. The noun form of the word always appears in the plural form and in the KJV is translated "tender mercy" once, "inward affection" once and "bowels" nine times. The verb form of the word occurs 12 times in the New Testament and is translated "compassion" each time. The verb form has the meaning of "have pity, feel sympathy."

As Paul considered his relationship with the Philippians, as far as the emotional response was concerned, he saw it as something far higher than human interaction. It was a display of affection that originated in Jesus Christ. The Philippians and Paul were experiencing what he had expressed in Romans 5:5: "And hope does not disappoint, because the love of God has been poured out within our hearts through the Holy Spirit who was given to us."

Although there was no mission board behind the Apostle Paul, there were believers who were vitally concerned about the progress of the gospel, and their hearts were knit together with Paul's in all that he did.

Chapter 4 – Discerning and Applying "Things That Really Matter"

And this I pray, that your love may abound still more and more in real knowledge and all discernment (1:9).

THE FREQUENCY OF Paul's praying is indicated in the word translated "pray," for it is in the present tense. The Greek present tense emphasizes continuous action. Paul's reference to prayer could thus be translated: "This I keep on praying." He didn't just pray a few times for the Philippians and then forget about them; he made it a habit to pray for them.

Paul specified what he prayed for concerning the Philippians: "That your love may abound still more and more in real knowledge and all discernment." These words are tremendously significant in the light of the contemporary emphasis on love. In some theological circles today love is emphasized to the extent that one draws the inference that it does not matter what you believe as long as you love others. A verse frequently cited is John 13:35, which records Christ's word to His disciples: "By this all men will know that you are My disciples, if you have love for one another." What is usually forgotten, however, is that Christ presupposed that the disciples believed the right things about Him. It is tremendously important for the one who believes right doctrine to express love toward others. But love should never be a substitute for right doctrine.

As Paul wrote to the Philippians, he did not say that he made it a practice to pray that they might love him more or that they might love others more but that their love might abound, or overflow, "in real knowledge and all discernment." The word translated "love" is *agapē* and refers to the highest kind of love—the kind that loves even when there is no response. It is the kind of love that seeks the highest good of the other person.

Paul heaped one superlative on top of another to emphasize the need for increasing love—"may abound still more and more." But this overflowing, abounding love was not a love without restrictions; it was to be a love "in real knowledge and in all discernment."

Paul was not impressed by those who had love or zeal without knowledge. Concerning his fellow Israelites, he said, "For I testify about them that they have a zeal for God, but not in accordance with knowledge" (Rom. 10:2). The Greek word translated "knowledge" is the same in Romans 10:2 as it is in Philippians 1:9. The word is *epignosis*, which is an intense form of the common word for "knowledge." In its intensive form, it refers to an advanced knowledge. Paul did not want the Philippians to remain at their present level of knowledge of the Lord, good as that level might have been for them at that time. He wanted them to advance in their knowledge of Jesus Christ, and he wanted their love to be expressed in accordance with this knowledge.

Paul was also concerned that the love of the Philippians might abound "in all discernment." The word translated "discernment" is *aisthēsis*, meaning "insight." It has to do with the application of knowledge, which results in discernment. Christians who are unable to discern are not mature and thus are not able to handle the solid food of the Word.

To such a group, the writer of Hebrews said, "For though by this time you ought to be teachers, you have need again for someone to teach you the elementary principles of the oracles of God, and you have come to need milk and not solid food. For everyone who partakes *only* of milk is not accustomed to the word of righteousness, for he is an infant. But solid food is for the mature, who because of practice have their senses trained to discern good and evil" (5:12-14).

These verses indicate that the way one becomes mature is by training the senses to discern. This means that believers must make it a habit to apply to their daily lives what they read in the Word of God. As this daily application is practiced, the believer grows in his ability to discern and thus becomes a mature Christian.

So we see from Philippians 1:9 that it is not enough to know factual information from the Bible; one must apply this information to himself and to the situations in which he finds himself.

So that you may approve the things that are excellent, in order to be sincere and blameless until the day of Christ (1:10).

This verse shows the results of a love that abounds in knowledge and discernment. The word translated "approve" is *dokimazō* and involves the idea of testing, or proving, for the purpose of approving. It was used in New Testament times of testing metals and coins to determine which ones came up to the proper standards and, therefore, were approved.

Notice what the Philippians were to approve: "Things that are excellent." The word translated "excellent" is *diapherō*, meaning "things that really matter" or "things that differ." This word further emphasized Paul's prayer that the love of the Philippians would abound in discernment. To discern is to distinguish things that differ. Paul wanted them not only to distinguish what differed but also to approve that which proved to be of the Lord.

Paul seemed to have more in mind than distinguishing good from evil; most likely he was concerned that the Philippians be able to distinguish between what was good and what was best. This involves knowing what the Lord's will is in any given situation and then being obedient to it. It is easy for a Christian to become distracted by being involved in that which is good but is not precisely the Lord's will for his life. Paul wanted the Philippians to be discerning in these matters, to test and then to approve that which was best.

Paul explained his reason for wanting them to discern in this way: "In order to be sincere and blameless until the day of Christ." The word "sincere" means much more than the opposite of insincere. The Greek word is *eilikrinēs*, meaning "pure." It is used only twice in the New Testament—here and in 2 Peter 3:1. The word refers to something found to be of unmixed substance when tested. In Philippians 1:10 this word emphasizes the believer's relationship with God.

The word "blameless" emphasizes the believer's relationship with others. This word is from *aproskopos*, meaning "blameless" or "giving no offense." The same word is translated "no offense" in 1 Corinthians 10:32, where Paul told believers, "Give no offense either to Jews or to Greeks or to the church of God." The believer is to live in such a way that his life will glorify the Lord and that he will be blameless before others.

Having been filled with the fruit of the righteousness which *comes* through Jesus Christ, to the glory and praise of God (1:11).

The "fruit of the righteousness" is those characteristics produced by righteousness. It is apparent to others when a believer is living in fellowship with Jesus Christ. Such a person evidences the fruit of the Spirit—love, joy, peace, patience, kindness, goodness, faithfulness, gentleness, self-control (Gal. 5:22-23).

Paul emphasized to the Philippians that this fruit did not originate by one's self-efforts, for he said, "Which *comes* through Jesus Christ." The fruits of righteousness are the characteristics of Christ's life seen through the believer when he is in fellowship with Christ. They originate with Christ, not in the believer's self-efforts.

The fruit of righteousness comes by means of Jesus Christ and are "to the glory and praise of God." The believer who evidences the fruit of righteousness magnifies God by the way he lives. When one is in fellowship with Christ, the characteristics of Christ's life will be evidenced through his life. The believer who magnifies God in this way fulfills Christ's command: "Let your light shine before men in such a way that they may see your good works, and glorify your Father who is in heaven" (Matt. 5:16).

Chapter 5 - Paul's Shackles Aid Gospel Outreach

Now I want you to know, brethren, that my circumstances have turned out for the greater progress of the gospel (1:12).

PAUL'S WORDS "I want you to know, brethren" indicate that he wanted to make sure the Philippians would not misunderstand his situation in relation to the gospel. No doubt some were exceedingly discouraged because of Paul's imprisonment. Perhaps they thought the gospel was being hindered because he was a prisoner of the Roman government.

Paul referred to the Philippian believers as "brethren," which revealed his close identification with them. His heart went out to them as he knew they were thinking of him and his circumstances.

But if any believers thought the gospel was being hindered because of Paul's imprisonment, they had their thinking corrected by Paul's words: "That my circumstances have turned out for the greater progress of the gospel." The words "which happened" are italicized in the King James Version, indicating that they were added by the translators to make a smooth rendering of the Greek idiom involved. "Have turned out" is the Greek perfect tense of "come" (*erchomai*). Paul was showing the results accomplished by the things which had happened to him.

Imagine the scope of details and past experiences to which Paul alluded in his expression "that my circumstances have turned out." He could have elaborated on what he had suffered for the sake of the gospel. However, his attention was not on himself but on what had been accomplished for the sake of the gospel. During the past three years, he had experienced imprisonment, harassment and even threats against his life. But Paul bypassed these details and, instead, emphasized that all of these difficulties had actually furthered, not hindered, the gospel. The word translated "progress" is a form of *prokopē*, meaning, "progress, advancement." The verb form of this Greek word was originally used of a pioneer cutting his way through brushwood. The analogy here is that the problems that had obstructed Paul had actually cleared the path—had made opportunities for the gospel to advance.

How interesting that the circumstances which the Philippian believers had thought might hinder the gospel had actually resulted in its advancement! This shows that a sovereign God can use circumstances to accomplish His will. So, instead of allowing the Philippians to mourn over what was happening to him, Paul wanted them to rejoice in the advancement of the gospel. We see how Paul's circumstances had furthered the gospel in the following verse:

So that my imprisonment in *the cause of* **Christ has become well known throughout the whole praetorian guard and to everyone else (1:13).**

It is quite possible that Paul was actually chained to a guard while he was in prison.

His bonds were "in Christ" since it was because of his identification with Christ that he was in prison. But to any who might have thought that Paul's confinement meant the gospel was not going out, Paul said that his bonds were "well known throughout the whole praetorian guard." The word translated "praetorian" is *praitōrion*, which referred to the imperial guard. Or it can mean the "governor's official residence." Probably the best supported meaning is the one which refers to the soldiers themselves, inasmuch as Paul was under their constant guard.

It is not difficult to imagine how the soldiers were affected by Paul. During his imprisonment other persons were allowed to visit him. After the visitors had left, the soldiers had probably asked questions and discussed with Paul what he had told his visitors.

Acts 28:30-31 refers to this same time in Paul's life: "And he stayed two full years in his own rented quarters and was welcoming all who came to him, preaching the kingdom of God and teaching concerning the Lord Jesus Christ with all openness, unhindered." Imagine how the soldiers must have watched Paul's life to see if there would be any inconsistency with his testimony! But because of Paul's imprisonment, the gospel and his response to his confinement became known throughout this group of the imperial guard.

Inasmuch as Paul was able to have visitors, which gave him opportunities to preach and teach, his bonds were also manifest "to everyone else" (Phil. 1:13). Instead of being frustrated and despondent over his confinement, Paul rejoiced that this actually helped to spread the gospel in ever-widening circles. Those in Rome, the capital of the empire, were learning about his situation and at the same time were also learning about the Lord Jesus Christ, whom Paul loved and served. Christians were especially affected by Paul's imprisonment. Paul said:

And that most of the brethren, trusting in the Lord because of my imprisonment, have far more courage to speak the word of God without fear (1:14).

The word translated "most" means "the greater sum" and, therefore, has a sense of "most" rather than just "many." The majority of those believers who knew about Paul's imprisonment were greatly benefited. Those previously timid in letting their identification with Christ be known began speaking out boldly.

This is the way it usually happens. Instead of making believers more timid, history indicates that persecution usually makes them bolder in their convictions for Christ. The Philippian believers may have been focusing too much attention on circumstances, but Paul's life proved that even imprisonment could not put an end to the outreach of the gospel. As they saw Paul's positive response to his confinement, they realized that they had a peace and security that the world could not take away. Therefore, they began to speak out more boldly for Jesus Christ.

The confidence of these believers had increased to the extent that they had "far more courage to speak the word of God without fear." They were courageously sharing the Word of God with others. Paul's situation had caused them to see that spiritual matters were of far more importance than physical concerns. What an encouragement this must have been to the Apostle Paul to realize that his Roman imprisonment had encouraged believers in a way in which he could have never helped them on his own.

Chapter 6 – Christ Preached Despite Mixed Motives

Some, to be sure, are preaching Christ even from envy and strife, but some also from good will (1:15).

PAUL MADE THESE comments about those who were more boldly preaching the gospel because of his imprisonment. He thought of them as two groups who were preaching for different reasons. The first group he mentioned preached Christ through "envy and strife," while the second preached Christ through "good will."

A key question is: Were both groups preaching the same gospel but with different motives? Or were they preaching different messages as well as preaching with different motives? Paul said that both groups preached Christ. If one group had been preaching the keeping of the Law as a means of salvation, Paul would surely have condemned the group for preaching "a different gospel" even as he did in Galatians 1:6. So the main difference between the two groups mentioned in Philippians 1:15 was not their message but their motives. Concerning their motives, Paul wrote:

The latter *do it* out of love, knowing that I am appointed for the defense of the gospel (1:16).

How refreshing it must have been to the Apostle Paul to realize that the latter group to which he referred was motivated by love. No doubt Paul had in mind this group's love for Christ and for the unsaved, but the context bears out that he was especially impressed with their love for him, inasmuch as he added: "knowing that I am appointed for the defense of the gospel." Because the other group did not love Paul, those in it sought to take advantage of his situation and bring pressure on him because of his imprisonment. This latter group, however, was helping to ease Paul's burdens while in prison by their bold proclamation of the gospel.

The word Paul used for "appointed" (*keimai*) drew an analogy between Paul and a sentry posted for duty. In this context the word is used metaphorically and has the sense of "being appointed" or "being destined" for the defense of the gospel. The word "defense" is from *apologia* and is the word from which "apologetics" is derived. The same word appears in Philippians 1:7, where it is also translated "defense."

The former proclaim Christ out of selfish ambition rather than from pure motives, thinking to cause me distress in my imprisonment (1:17).

The word translated "selfish ambition" is *eritheia*, meaning "strife." Paul also indicated they were not preaching sincerely, and for this he used *hagnōs*, meaning "purely." This group did not have pure motives as they preached Christ. The motives these people had are implied by Paul in the last statement of verse 17: "Thinking to cause me distress in my imprisonment." This group sought to rouse friction for Paul by preaching the gospel. These people were apparently jealous of Paul, and now that he was in prison, they saw their opportunity to advance their own cause. At the same time they hoped to add to his distress and frustration in prison.

This is a reminder of the professional jealousy today even between many evangelical churches. Although almost all give lip service to serving the same Christ and to preaching the same gospel, there is often an underlying selfish ambition to outdo other churches.

No doubt this is the basis for the great emphasis on numbers in most churches. Even though churches should be concerned with reaching as many people as possible, sometimes one wonders if the real motive for emphasizing attendance figures is not to show how one group has been more successful than other groups in reaching people. But numbers alone do not indicate spiritual success. Church leaders need to be very careful that they are not proclaiming the right message with the wrong motives.

Bible students using the King James Version will observe that verses 16 and 17 appear in reverse order. This is because these verses are found in different order in various Greek manuscripts, but the content is the same regardless of the order. Notice Paul's response to the two groups preaching the same message but with different motives:

What then? Only that in every way, whether in pretense or in truth, Christ is proclaimed; and in this I rejoice. Yes, and I will rejoice. (1:18).

"Pretense" is literally "falsely alleged motive" or "pretext." Even though Paul realized that the motives of one group were definitely wrong, he still rejoiced that Christ was being preached, and he would continue to rejoice in this, even if their motives continued to be wrong. This is one statement that most Bible students probably wish Paul would have expanded so they could apply it better to situations they face. But Paul, writing by the inspiration of the Holy Spirit, was content to leave it without explanation. Paul's statement serves as a vivid reminder that believers should rejoice when Christ is proclaimed, regardless of secondary issues that do not honor Him.

Chapter 7 – Results of Paul's Imprisonment

For I know that this will turn out for my deliverance through your prayers and the provision of the Spirit of Jesus Christ (1:19).

AS PAUL WAS in jail, he was thrilled to realize that as a result of his personal imprisonment the name of Christ was now being more widely proclaimed than ever. Some were preaching because of wrong motives, but Paul was still pleased to realize that people were hearing about Jesus Christ.

Apparently it was this wider proclamation of Christ to which Paul referred when he said, "This will turn out for my deliverance." The word translated "deliverance" is the common word that is used throughout the New Testament. However, the word does not always refer to spiritual salvation, as it is generally used today in evangelical circles. It was also used to refer to the healing of the body.

Matthew 9:21 records a woman's statement concerning Christ: "If I only touch His garment, I will get well." The word translated "well" is the verb form of the word translated "deliverance" in Philippians 1:19. The word was also used of one's well-being. It is translated "save" and refers to well-being in Mark 15:30 where it is recorded that those around the cross told Jesus, "Save yourself, and come down from the cross!"

In Philippians 1:19 the subject was not spiritual salvation, for Paul had been saved spiritually for some time. Neither was the subject physical healing; rather, it was his well-being as he was in prison. Perhaps Paul saw the possibility of his release from prison, although it seems sufficient from the text to understand that Paul was talking about the preaching of the gospel being to his benefit while he was in prison.

Paul was aware of the means God was using to bring about his benefit. He told the Philippians, "Through your prayers and the provision of the Spirit of Jesus Christ." This reveals the confidence Paul had in the prayers of fellow believers, and it also reveals his dependency on the Holy Spirit.

The word translated "provision" is *epichorēgia*. The word means "supply" in the sense of "support." The Holy Spirit was referred to by the Lord Jesus as the *paraklētos* (John 14:16,26; 15:26; 16:7). By this name the Holy Spirit is seen as the One called alongside to help, and Paul was experiencing His support while in prison. Paul went on to say:

According to my earnest expectation and hope, that I will not be put to shame in anything, but *that* with all boldness, Christ will even now, as always, be exalted in my body, whether by life or by death (1:20).

The words "earnest expectation" are translated from *apokaradokian*, which literally meant "to watch with the head stretched out." It was used in secular writing of a watchman who kept looking into the darkness for the first gleam of a distant beacon. With this same anticipation and with hope, Paul looked forward to not being ashamed in anything. His desire was to glorify Jesus Christ in all that he did, whether in prison or out.

Paul's imprisonment had given others a boldness to proclaim Jesus Christ, and in verse 20 it is evident that Paul himself had a boldness even in prison. Although the Roman government could confine him physically, they could not confine the gospel, nor could they stop Paul from witnessing by his words and his life.

So great was his desire to glorify Christ that Paul said, "Christ will even now, as always, be exalted in my body, whether by life or by death."

Paul hoped to be delivered from prison, but even if he never was, this would not keep him from magnifying Jesus Christ. The word translated "exalted" is *megalunō*, meaning, "to make large." It is used in a figurative sense to mean "exalt" or "glorify." Paul's body was confined in a prison, but he was determined to use it to reveal Christ to others in a way they had never seen before. Paul realized that death could take place if the Roman government chose to execute him, but he was determined to use his body to glorify Christ, even if he were sentenced to death.

This verse emphasizes that the unsaved can see Christ only as He is revealed through believers. The Lord Jesus Christ does not come down to earth to walk among people, but He lives within believers and wants to express Himself through their bodies. Since nothing can really be done apart from the body, Paul told believers, "Therefore I urge you, brethren, by the mercies of God, to present your bodies a living and holy sacrifice, acceptable to God, *which is* your spiritual service of worship" (Rom. 12:1).

Paul's concern was to have his body act as a magnifying glass for the Lord Jesus Christ so that others could see the characteristics of Christ. If he were freed from prison, he would be able to do this in the way he lived. But even if death came, he was determined to magnify Christ, even in the act of death. Paul summarized all of his thinking on this matter by his great statement:

For to me, to live is Christ and to die is gain (1:21).

Paul equated living with Jesus Christ. Paul was so conscious of the grace that God had manifested to him that he could not conceive of life apart from Jesus Christ. So, to Paul, living meant being taken up with Jesus Christ. The burning desire of Paul's heart was to "know Him and the power of His resurrection" (3:10).

Death, however, would bring an even greater benefit for the Apostle Paul. He said, "To die is gain." The word translated "gain" is *kerdos* and meant "gain" in the sense of "profit." It was used in the secular writing of Paul's day to refer to interest that money had gained.

Paul realized that there would be much profit to him spiritually after he died because he would then be in the very presence of Jesus Christ.

Paul did not endeavor to make the act of dying a beautiful experience, but as he looked beyond death he saw all the benefits he would have and, therefore, was able to say "to die is gain." Every person who knows Jesus Christ as personal Savior may have the same confidence the Apostle Paul had.

Chapter 8 – Departing or Staying: God's Choice

But if *I am* to live *on* in the flesh, this *will mean* fruitful labor for me; and I do not know which to choose (1:22).

IN THIS PASSAGE, Paul was contrasting living in the body with living in the presence of Christ. Whichever the case, he had determined to magnify Christ in his body "whether by life or by death" (v. 20).

In verse 22 Paul was using the term "flesh" to refer to his body. The Greek word translated "flesh" (*sarx*) could be used to refer either to the sinful adamic nature or to the body itself. It was used to refer to the sin nature in such verses as Romans 7:18: "For I know nothing good dwells in me, that is, in my flesh; for the willing is present in me, but the doing of the good *is* not." Galatians 5:17 also used the word "flesh" in referring to the sin nature: "For the flesh sets its desire against the Spirit, and the Spirit against the flesh; for these are in opposition to one another, so that you may not do the things that you please."

However, the word translated "flesh" was used to refer to the body in such verses as Galatians 2:20: "I have been crucified with Christ; and it is no longer I who live, but Christ lives in me; and the *life* which I now live in the flesh I live by faith in the Son of God, who loved me and gave Himself up for me."

Since *sarx* could be used either of the old nature or the body, one must examine the context of Philippians 1:22 carefully to see which was intended. The clue is found in verse 20 where Paul referred to magnifying Christ "in my body." The passage emphasized only whether Paul would remain in the body to be with the Philippians or would leave his body to be with Christ.

As Paul set forth the alternatives, he said, "If *I am* to live on in the flesh, this *will mean* fruitful labor for me." The phrase "this *will mean* fruitful labor for me" was written in brief form, and Paul expected the reader to supply the thought. Paul wanted the reader to understand that if he remained in the body, it meant he would have fruit for his labor. He realized that by staying with the Philippians and other believers, more fruit would result from his work with them, whereas no further fruit would result if he died, left the body and entered the presence of the Lord.

As to which he personally desired most, he said, "And I do not know which to choose." Whether to remain or to go to be with the Lord—Paul admitted that this was a difficult choice to make if left up to him. As he wrote this letter from prison, he realized that his life was in jeopardy and that he might soon be in the presence of the Lord, regardless of personal choice. But if the choice were left up entirely to him, he would have difficulty in deciding, since his heart was drawn to the Philippians as well as to the Lord. He went on to explain in the following verse:

But I am hard-pressed from both *directions*, having the desire to depart and be with Christ, for that is very much better (1:23).

The word Paul used for "hard-pressed" was *sunechō*, and in this context it means, "distressed." It was difficult for him to choose what would be best for everyone concerned.

It meant deciding either to remain with the Philippians to build them up in the faith or to personally experience the blessedness of going into the presence of the Lord.

As to his personal desires, he said, "Having the desire to depart and be with Christ, for that is very much better." The word translated "depart" was the same word Paul used in the final New Testament letter he penned. There he said, "For I already being poured out as a drink offering, and the time of my departure has come" (2 Tim. 4:6). Both in his letter to Timothy and in his letter to the Philippians, Paul referred to physical death by this word, used in secular Greek for the untying of tent ropes from the stakes in preparation for moving on. Paul viewed death as a loosening of those ties which held him to this life and the freedom to move into the presence of Christ.

Such a departure from this life would make it possible for Paul "to be with Christ." From Paul's writings we learn that all believers are in Christ, but Paul desired to be with Christ. When a person trusts Jesus Christ as personal Savior, he is placed into the Body of Christ by the Holy Spirit (see 1 Cor. 12:13). Therefore, each believer is in Christ. This expression is used only of Church-age believers; it is never stated that Old Testament saints were "in Christ."

But Paul looked forward to that time when he would be with Christ, which he said "is very much better." It would be far better for Paul because he would be loosed from the hindrances of this life that had caused him so much suffering and anguish. But it would not be better as far as the Philippians were concerned because they were in need of spiritual strengthening and encouragement. This is why Paul went on to say:

Yet to remain on in the flesh is more necessary for your sake (1:24).

Although Paul would have been personally better-off with Christ, he realized that for the sake of the Philippians it was better that he remain in the body. Paul was confident that the Lord would not take him home at this time because his work on earth was not yet finished. Here again we see Paul's custom of putting others before himself. He had gone through so much and would have been so relieved to be loosed from this life and to enter into the presence of the Lord, where there would be no pain or sorrow. But because he realized others needed what he could provide, Paul was content to remain in this life and to keep on enduring its hardships.

Chapter 9 – Words of Hope and Caution

AS PAUL WROTE to the believers in Philippi, did he think he would be released from prison? What characteristics did Paul especially want to see evidenced in the lives of the Philippians? These questions are answered in Philippians 1:25-27. Paul wrote:

Convinced of this, I know that I will remain and continue with you all for your progress and joy in the faith (1:25).

The words "convinced of this" referred to what Paul had just written: "To remain on in the flesh is more necessary for your sake" (v. 24). Although Paul wanted to be released from his body so he could go directly to be with the Lord, he realized this was not the best at that time because of the Philippian believers.

Having been assured that the Lord wanted him in the body in order to be of encouragement to the Philippians, Paul wrote: "Convinced of this, I know that I will remain and continue with you" (v. 25). The definiteness of Paul's confidence is seen in that the word translated "convinced of this" occurs in the Greek perfect tense. This tense emphasizes something that has been completed in the past but has a continuing effect. It was as if Paul were saying to the Philippians: "I will remain and continue with all of you for your progress and joy in the faith" (v. 25). The words "remain" and "continue" seem so alike on the surface that one wonders why Paul used both. However, he made a delicate distinction that is not seen in the English words. The word translated "remain" is *menō*, meaning "to remain" or "to stay." The word translated "continue" is *paramenō*. The end of this word is *menō* and has the same basic meaning; however, the first part of the word (*para*) emphasizes "alongside of." So Paul was stressing that he would remain alongside of these believers and thus be of spiritual help to them.

Paul assured the Philippians that he would remain alongside of them for their "progress and joy in the faith" (v. 25). The word translated "progress" is *prokopē*, meaning, "advancement." This is the same word translated "progress" in verse 12 of this same chapter. Paul's remaining with the Philippians would result in their spiritual progress, and advancement. His remaining with them would also add to their "joy in the faith." They were believers in Christ, and no one could take away what they had in Christ, but having Paul alongside to encourage and to instruct them would give them added joy.

So that your proud confidence in me may abound in Christ Jesus through my coming to you again (1:26).

This verse also reveals the result of Paul's remaining with the Philippians. It would cause their rejoicing to "abound." They were already rejoicing because of what they had in Christ, but Paul's remaining with them would cause them to rejoice even more.

Notice that their abundant rejoicing was focused "in Christ Jesus." The Philippians realized that the only true source of joy is Jesus Christ. The things of this world satisfy for a time, but true joy and contentment are found only in Christ.

Paul alluded to their more abundant joy as also being associated with his coming to them—"through my coming to you again." Imagine how thrilled these Philippian believers would be to see Paul again! When he was in Philippi, he was beaten and thrown into prison (see Acts 16:23-29). The Philippians had gained much spiritually from Paul, and now they were grieving for him because he was in prison in Rome. But what a reunion it would be when they saw him again!

Having stressed the joy that would be involved in their meeting again, Paul urged the Philippians to give serious attention to the way they were living for the Lord.

Only conduct yourselves in a manner worthy of the gospel of Christ, so that whether I come and see you or remain absent, I will hear of you that you are standing firm in one spirit, with one mind striving together for the faith of the gospel (1:27).

The word translated "conduct" is *politeuomai*, meaning "to live, conduct oneself, lead one's life." This same word appears in Acts 23:1, where it is translated "have lived." The noun form of this word is found in Philippians 3:20.

Paul was concerned that the Philippian believers live in a way that would glorify Jesus Christ. In particular, he wanted their conduct to be "in a manner worthy of the gospel of Christ." The believer's life should "adorn the doctrine of God our Savior in every respect" (Titus 2:10). When a Christian lives in a way that is becoming to the gospel, he will attract others to Jesus Christ. A believer is responsible to know more than just the right information; he is to live in accordance with that information. But one must know the right information in order to live the right way.

The "gospel of Christ" (Phil. 1:27) referred specifically to the good news of all that Jesus Christ had done for mankind. The Apostle Paul particularly spelled out the content of the gospel in 1 Corinthians 15:1-8—the death, burial and resurrection of Jesus Christ and the eyewitness reports of these things. Because of all that the Lord Jesus Christ has done for him, the believer is to live in a way that will magnify Jesus Christ in all that he does.

Although Paul hoped to see the Philippians soon, he was concerned that, whether he appeared or not, the Philippians would glorify Christ and "standing firm in one spirit, with one mind striving together for the faith of the gospel." The one spirit mentioned here probably refers to attitude rather than the Holy Spirit. What the believer's attitude should be is mentioned specifically in Chapter 2. Paul was concerned that the believers have unity of mind, or "one spirit," in all that they did for Jesus Christ.

Paul also added: "With one mind striving together for the faith of the gospel." The word translated "striving together" emphasized people fighting alongside of each other for a common cause. The common cause of the Philippian believers was "the faith of the gospel." This body of truth which made up the Christian faith was what the Philippian believers were to contend for with all of their strength. And they were also to live in such a way as to glorify Jesus Christ, in whom that faith was centered.

Chapter 10 – Suffering for His Sake

In no way alarmed by *your* opponents—which is a sign of destruction for them, but of salvation for you, and that *too*, from God (1:28).

HAVING TOLD THE Philippian believers, "With one mind striving together for the faith of the gospel" (v. 27), Paul then urged them not to overreact when they faced opposition.

The word translated "alarmed" (*pturō*) means "to frighten" or, in the passive voice, "to let oneself be intimidated." The word had the element of sudden fear inasmuch as the verb was used of horses being frightened. Paul did not want the Philippian believers to be like a high-strung horse that shies at every strange movement.

Paul said, "In no way alarmed by *your* opponents." The Philippians could be assured of the fact that there would be adversaries. Those who take a strong opinion for Jesus Christ will run into opposition. It is a principle of the Christian life that anyone who determines to "live godly in Christ Jesus will be persecuted" (2 Tim. 3:12).

The Philippians could remember how Paul and Silas reacted when they were beaten and thrown into prison in Philippi (Acts 16:23-29). Instead of being terrified, Paul and Silas prayed and sang praises to God at midnight (v. 25). What an impression this must have made on the other prisoners who heard them!

Because of the potential impact on others, Paul did not

want the Philippians to be terrified by anything. He said that their lack of terror would be "a sign of destruction" (Phil. 1:28) to the unbelievers. If those who opposed the Philippian believers saw that they were not easily shaken, it would even further convince them of their own lost condition, or "destruction" (*apōleia*), meaning "ruin." This verse emphasizes the importance of a believer's not suddenly reacting, or overreacting, when an unbeliever raises an objection to the Christian faith. If the believer immediately expresses fear, it gives the indication that he is unsure of the Christian faith, and this will cause the unsaved person to take comfort in his own unbelief.

This raises the question, If the believer has the tendency to be suddenly frightened every time he meets opposition to his faith, how does he overcome it? A probable reason for fright in a situation like this is that the believer is afraid he'll be challenged on a point which he can't satisfactorily defend. The Christian may have the feeling that if he cannot adequately answer the question, the whole cause of Christianity will be weakened.

It is important to remember, however, that some questions are impossible to answer and that sometimes a questioner is not really looking for an answer. But Christianity is true whether or not a believer can give a satisfactory answer to a specific question. Every believer should be faithful in his study so that he's ready to give a defense at any time (1 Pet. 3:15), but he must not be under the impression that he has to satisfactorily answer every question that is raised. He should, however, be willing to find the answer and report back to those who oppose him if they are sincere in wanting an answer.

Quite likely the opposition Paul referred to had to do with far more than questions or antagonistic comments; there was probably the threat of physical abuse. But if the Philippians could maintain their composure in the face of these threats, it would further convince the unsaved of the certainty of coming judgments on themselves.

Whereas a Christian's unshaken attitude is an evidence to the unbelievers of their destruction, it is an evidence to the believer of his salvation. Paul said, "But of salvation for you, and that *too*, from God." When a Christian, in the face of opposition, relies on the power of the Holy Spirit and remains unshaken, he realizes that this is an evidence of his salvation because he wouldn't have the strength in himself to do this. How wonderful for the believer to know that Jesus Christ is with him always, regardless of the circumstances (see Matt. 28:20; Heb. 13:5).

The reason believers should not be startled, or terrified, by their adversaries is given in verse 29:

For to you it has been granted for Christ's sake, not only to believe in Him, but also to suffer for His sake (1:29).

When believers realize that suffering in behalf of Christ is a part of their Christianity, they will not be startled, or terrified, when it comes. Two elements in verse 29 were presented by Paul as privileges: "Not only to believe in Him, but also to suffer for His sake."

What a tremendous privilege it is to have forgiveness of sin and eternal life by believing in the Lord Jesus Christ as one's personal Savior. This presupposes that a person recognizes that he is a sinner and deserving of God's condemnation or else he would not realize his need to receive Christ as Savior in the first place. But upon transferring his trust from himself and what he can do to Jesus Christ and what He has done for him, a person becomes a child of God and is delivered from condemnation (see John 1:12; 5:24).

But notice the other privilege that Paul mentioned in Philippians 1:29: "But also to suffer for His sake." Suffering in itself is not a privilege, but it is a privilege to suffer in behalf of the Lord Jesus Christ. A person guilty of wrongdoing suffers at the hands of others for his wrongdoing. But when he has not done wrong and yet is suffering for Christ, this is a distinct privilege (see 1 Pet. 2:19-20).

This also reveals that not all suffering is due to committing some sin. Jesus had to correct His disciples' thinking on this concerning the man born blind (see John 9:1-4). They thought that his condition was caused either by his sin or by his parents' sin. Jesus explained to them that neither was the case but that his blindness was for the purpose of revealing the works of God in him.

As the Philippians suffered for the sake of Christ, the works of God would also be revealed in them. God would be magnified through their lives.

Experiencing the same conflict which you saw in me, and now hear *to be* in me (1:30).

The word translated "conflict" (*agōn*) means "struggle" or "fight." Paul's thought here apparently went back to what was said in verse 27, where he told the Philippians to strive together for the faith of the gospel. Paul viewed all Christians to be in a serious conflict where they needed to fight shoulder to shoulder against the enemy.

"Experiencing the same conflict which you saw in me" probably referred to his experiences in Philippi when he was beaten and imprisoned. He had been persecuted there as he preached the gospel, and now these Philippians were also being persecuted. Perhaps earlier they had a difficult time identifying with Paul in what he was experiencing, but now they would have no difficulty because of what they themselves were going through.

Paul added: "And now hear *to be* in me." He was writing this letter from a prison in Rome, and the Philippians had heard what he was undergoing. The Philippians in behalf of Paul undoubtedly offered many prayers during his Roman imprisonment. Inasmuch as the Philippians were now companions in suffering, they could pray with far greater understanding concerning Paul's situation. This kind of fellowship in suffering and prayer was always of tremendous encouragement to Paul.

Chapter 11 – Bases of Spiritual Unity

Therefore if there is any encouragement in Christ, if there is any consolation of love, if there is any fellowship of the Spirit, if any affection and compassion (2:1).

IT IS DIFFICULT to imagine any greater difference between New Testament Greek and present-day English than what is seen in the "if" clauses in this verse. In English, "if" presents a condition that may or may not be true. However, in the Greek language the way the "if" clauses are used in this verse assumes the condition to be true.

So one could read this verse, "If there is any encouragement in Christ, and there is," or "Because there is encouragement in Christ," and so on.

Paul had written to the Philippians: "Only conduct yourselves in a manner worthy of the gospel of Christ, so that whether I come and see you or remain absent, I will hear of you that you are standing firm in one spirit, with one mind striving together for the faith of the gospel" (1:27). Then, he exhorted them to manifest spiritual unity because of the various things that are true, which are listed in 2:1.

The word translated "encouragement" is *paraklēsis*, meaning "exhortation." The word involves more than comfort or consolation. This Greek word is related to the one used in referring to the Holy Spirit (*paraklētos*), meaning "helper." Sometimes the help needed is comfort, while at other times it is conviction or rebuke. But whatever is needed, the Holy

Spirit is able to supply. Because all of this is available in Christ, Paul saw this as a basis for appealing to the Philippians for spiritual unity.

To this first part of Philippians 2:1 Paul added: "If any consolation of love." Since the consolation (comfort or exhortation) of love is available, this, too, is a basis for spiritual unity. When one knows Jesus Christ as personal Savior, his attitude changes toward other people. Love is a fruit of the Spirit (Gal. 5:22), and the individual who walks in fellowship with the Lord reveals the fruit of the Spirit.

The word translated "love" in both Galatians 5:22 and Philippians 2:1 is *agapē*. This word emphasizes an act of the will whereby the individual seeks the highest good of another. Even though there might be matters in the local church at Philippi that Christians would be in disagreement about, they were responsible to seek each other's highest good in whatever they did. This kind of love produces consolation, or comfort, and that honors Jesus Christ.

Paul's third basis in appealing to the Philippian believers for spiritual unity was the "fellowship of the Spirit." This was a divine *koinōnia*. It was a fellowship that had its origin in the Holy Spirit, the One who brings about spiritual unity.

In this day when stress is placed on organizational unity, it is important to realize that Paul was talking about a spiritual unity, not an organizational one. It is regrettable that people have sometimes become involved in organizational unity where there is no spiritual unity because they do not believe what the Bible says about the Person and work of Jesus Christ. Inasmuch as the Holy Spirit's ministry is to reveal Jesus Christ (John 16:14), no believers should expect spiritual unity with others unless there is common agreement about the Person and work of Christ.

Paul's fourth appeal for spiritual unity was because of "affection and compassion." Whereas today it is common to regard the heart as the seat of emotions, in Bible times the bowels were considered such. Paul was here appealing to the affections that the Holy Spirit had placed within believers in regard to other believers. Having concern for others is one of the greatest indications among believers that a person is in a right relationship with Jesus Christ. The believer who is unconcerned for others is a carnal Christian (1 Cor. 3:3), for he is living to satisfy his fleshly desires rather than seeking to please Christ and to be considerate of others.

From Philippians 2:1 we see as Dr. John F. Walvoord wrote that "a Christian who is exhorted by Christ, encouraged by the knowledge of His love, experiencing fellowship of the Holy Spirit, and possessing a true heart of compassion and attitude of mercy is equipped to realize spiritual unity" (*Philippians: Triumph in Christ*, p. 50).

Make my joy complete by being of the same mind, maintaining the same love, united in spirit, intent on one purpose (2:2).

Having stated the bases for spiritual unity, Paul appealed to the believers to fulfill his joy by expressing their unity in specific ways.

The word "make" has the sense of "fulfill." Paul took joy in the Philippian believers, and he wanted them to fill his joy full by evidencing their spiritual unity. A word that Paul used often in his letter to the Philippians was "joy" (*chara*), even though he was writing from a Roman prison. Paul was able to have joy in the midst of these adverse circumstances because he knew that God was going to accomplish His perfect will. Paul was thrilled with the response of the believers in Philippi, but he urged them to fill his joy full by manifesting spiritual unity.

Specifically, Paul exhorted the Philippian believers: "being of the same mind." "Same mind" is a translation of three Greek words, literally meaning, "to think the same thing." Paul's imperative was in the Greek present tense, emphasizing continuous action, or a practice. Thus, he was exhorting the believers to keep on thinking the same thing.

Does this expression mean that there is never to be a disagreement? It is unreasonable to push this expression to this extent. Because individuals have different backgrounds and view things differently, it is only normal to expect differing opinions on certain subjects. Believers are to be agreed on basic matters. If those in the local church are agreed on the doctrinal issues of the Person and work of Christ and have the same goals in mind for their group, they will have harmony, even though occasionally there will be differences of opinion on how to reach those goals. Paul was concerned that there be a unity of thinking and that the Philippian believers keep on thinking in this way.

"Maintaining the same love" was a quality Paul wanted the Philippian believers to possess along with their unity in thinking. In fact, these two are so closely linked that it's impossible to conceive how there could be unity in thinking if the believers did not possess the same love. But as the believers made it a way of life to seek each other's highest good, they would also have unity in thinking. "United in spirit, intent on one purpose" emphasizes the harmony of the group. The word translated "one purpose" is a combination of the Greek words meaning "together" and "soul." They were to be of one soul, which stresses again the unity which Paul wanted them to have.

Paul also urged them to be "of the same mind," which again involved the thinking process. These elements tend to overlap each other as Paul emphasized the importance of believers expressing unity and harmony because of all that they have in Christ, as alluded to in verse 1.

Chapter 12 –
Cultivating Genuine
Concern for Others

Do nothing from selfishness or empty conceit, but with humility of mind regard one another as more important than yourselves (2:3).

AS PAUL WROTE to the Philippian believers to encourage them in a harmonious relationship with each other, he exhorted them to do nothing "from selfishness or empty conceit." The word translated "selfishness" (*eritheia*) has the sense of "selfish ambition." This same word was used by Paul as he listed some of the works of the flesh in Galatians 5: "idolatry, sorcery, enmities, strife [*eritheia*], jealousy, outbursts of anger, disputes, dissensions, factions" (v. 20).

Believers who pursue selfish ambition are carnal Christians (see 1 Cor. 3:3). Paul did not want them to do anything through "empty conceit." The Greek word *kenodoxia* literally means "empty glory." This is the only time this form occurs in the New Testament, although a related form (*kenodoxos*) occurs in Galatians 5:26 and is translated "boastful." It seems that strife and boasting are related because believers who pursue selfish ambition achieve only an empty glory.

In contrast to doing anything through selfishness or empty conceit, Paul told the Philippian believers, "But with humility of mind regard one another as more important than yourselves." Of two different conjunctions Paul could have used to show contrast, he used the stronger of the two here. "Humility of mind" is a translation of the one Greek word *tapeinophrosunē*, which has the meaning of "modesty." Rather than pursuing selfish ambition, Paul wanted the believers to evidence modesty about themselves in their relationship to others.

This would be accomplished as they heeded Paul's injunction: "Regard one another as more important than yourselves." The word translated "regard" (*hēgeomai*), has the meaning of "think" or "consider." This was Paul's way of telling the Philippian believers that they should put others first in all of their relationships. Paul's first letter to the Corinthians shows what happens when believers don't do this, for the church at Corinth had been deeply affected by self-seeking Christians.

How is a believer to regard other believers as better than himself? The Greek word Paul used (*huperechō*) contained the element of superiority, for it meant "to surpass" or "to excel." The Christian in right relationship with the Lord treats others as if they were his superiors. When He was on earth, Jesus told His followers: "And whoever wishes to be first among you shall be your slave; just as the Son of Man did not come to be served, but to serve, and to give His life a ransom for many" (Matt. 20:27-28).

Do not merely look out for your own personal interests, but also for the interests of others (2:4).

These words are closely linked to the preceding statement. Those who regard others as better than themselves are those who are not just looking out for themselves but who are concerned for others. The believer who is living in fellowship with Jesus Christ is not self-centered but has a genuine concern for others. It is contrary to one's basic nature to be concerned for others, inasmuch as the old nature, the adamic nature, is selfish.

But the one who has trusted Jesus Christ as Savior is to be characterized by a genuine concern for others. And the concern that one believer has for other believers will even have an impact on non-Christians. Jesus said, "By this all men will know that you are My disciples, if you have love for one another" (John 13:35).

Rather than promoting self, the believer is to be genuinely concerned about others and to promote their interests. Because this is so different from human nature, such an attitude will be a witness to unbelievers. But such an attitude is possible only as a believer appreciates the grace which God has bestowed on him. As he recognizes that all he has is a result of the grace of God, it will not be difficult for a believer to put others first.

Chapter 13 – Same Attitude as Jesus

Have this attitude in yourselves which was also in Christ Jesus (2:5).

THE WORD TRANSLATED "attitude" in this verse is *phroneō* and is translated "to feel" in 1:7 and "same mind" and "one purpose" in 2:2. The word stresses the thinking process. One who thinks in a certain way is one who is spoken of as having a certain type of mind. In what way is the Christian to think? What kind of a mind is he to have? Paul said the believer was to think in the same way as Christ, or to have the same kind of mind that Jesus Christ had (v. 5).

Paul was concerned that the Philippian believers—and all Christians—have the same attitude that Jesus Christ had. One could make a study of the Bible, gleaning from its pages the different characteristics of the attitude of Jesus Christ, but Paul had his own specific illustration as he wrote to the Philippians. Having said, "Have this attitude in yourselves which was also in Christ Jesus," the question that could naturally be expected is, What kind of attitude was this? Verses 6-8 reveal how Jesus Christ thought. Although this section is primarily an illustration to show believers how they ought to think, it is one of the most significant theological passages in the Bible.

Who, although He existed in the form of God, did not regard equality with God a thing to be grasped (2:6).

The key word in this verse is the one which is translated "form." The word is *morphē*, which appears three times in the New Testament (Mark 16:12; Phil. 2:6-7) and is translated "form" in each case. The Greek word emphasizes the inner essence of a person or thing. Thus, Paul was telling the Philippians that when Jesus Christ was with the Father before He came to earth, He had the inner essence of God. Paul would never have consented to any teaching that made Jesus Christ less than God. Many in Paul's day (and many today) did not believe that Jesus Christ was God. But Jesus Christ was not only God before He came to earth, but even while He was on earth He claimed that He was equal with God. If He had claimed to be less than God, He would not have so disturbed the leaders of the Jews. But they clearly understood what His claims were. John 5:18 says, "For this reason therefore the Jews were seeking all the more to kill Him, because He not only was breaking the Sabbath, but also was calling God His own Father, making Himself equal with God." Even though some today refuse to believe that Jesus Christ is God and that He is equal with the Father, the Jewish leaders clearly understood His claims, and this is why they hated Him so bitterly.

Even though Christ, as to His inner essence, is God, He "did not regard equality with God a thing to be grasped" (2:6). From this verse it is apparent that there was some element of Jesus' equality with God that He was willing to give up. One cannot give up the qualities of his inner nature, but he can relinquish the right, in some respects, to outwardly express his inner nature. Even though Christ was God Himself and had the right to display His attributes, He willingly gave up this right in order to come to earth to be the Savior of the world. He did not cease being in the form of God as to His inner nature, but He gave up being equal with God as far as the expression of some of His attributes was concerned.

Chapter 14 – From Glory to the Cross

THE PHILIPPIAN CHRISTIANS were to have the same mind in them that was in Christ Jesus (Phil. 2:5). In telling them this, the Apostle Paul explained the kind of attitude that characterized the Lord Jesus Christ. Although as to His form (v. 6) He was God, He did not consider it something to be grasped in order to maintain the glory He had with the Father.

But emptied Himself, taking the form of a bond-servant, *and* being made in the likeness of men (2:7).

The emptying of Himself was the opposite of grasping after what He had in the presence of the Father—independent exercise of authority and the free expression of His attributes. Thus, it could be said that Jesus "emptied Himself."

Instead, He "[took] the form of a bond-servant." The word translated "form" is *morphē*, the same word translated "form" in verse 6. As to His inner essence, He was God, but upon His choice to come to earth, He took on also the inner essence of a servant. The word Paul used for "bond-servant" was the common word in New Testament times for "slave."

What a contrast! Jesus Christ gave up the highest glory imaginable—a position of complete independence—and took the lowest position thinkable. A bond-servant, or a slave, is the one who has no will of his own but is entirely subjected to serving the will of another. Jesus Christ came to earth to do the will of His Father and, at the end of His earthly life, was able to say to the Father, "I glorified You on the earth, having accomplished the work which You have given Me to do" (John 17:4). The love of the Lord Jesus Christ for fallen man is indicated by the fact that He would not have had to give up His position of glory and take on the form of a servant. He could have insisted on His right to retain the glory He had with the Father. This is the exact point Paul was making to the Philippians. Although it was the right of the Lord Jesus Christ to retain this position He had with the Father, He willingly gave it up for others.

In being willing to give up His position of glory, the Lord Jesus Christ was "made in the likeness of men." These words reveal His identification with mankind, for His appearance was similar.

Being found in appearance as a man, He humbled Himself by becoming obedient to the point of death, even death on a cross (2:8).

A key word in this verse is the one translated "appearance" (*schēma*), which emphasizes the outer appearance. As to His inner essence, Christ was the God-Man, but outwardly He appeared "as a man." So much did He appear as a man that many of His contemporaries did not know He was also God.

In this passage, which emphasizes what the Lord Jesus Christ gave up, Paul said, "He humbled Himself." The Lord Jesus Christ was willing to be born into a family of low estate. It was one thing for Him to be willing to give up His glory with the Father and to be born into the human race, but it was quite another thing for Him to be willing to be born into a family which had very little of this world's goods. He could have chosen to be born into the family of the Roman Emperor, thereby assuring Himself of eventually ruling the then-known world.

By being born into any Roman family, thus being a Roman citizen, he would have been protected from the most horrible form of execution—crucifixion. This was reserved for non-Romans and even then for only the grossest of criminals. But Jesus Christ willingly gave up the glory He had with the Father and became a member of a family existing on the level of poverty. What a lesson His example was to the first-century Philippian Christians, and what a lesson it ought to be to 21st-century Christians.

Jesus Christ "[became] obedient to the point of death, even death on a cross." It is difficult enough to imagine the Lord Jesus Christ giving up His glory with the Father and taking a position that would involve death, but it is especially difficult to imagine that He would agree to experience "the death on a cross." Even the unsaved in Philippi, with their Greek culture, probably shuddered at the thought of the ugly death on a cross, and Paul told the believers that this is precisely what Jesus Christ chose in contrast to His former position. No wonder the Apostle John said, "In this is love, not that we loved God, but that He loved us and sent His Son *to be* the propitiation for our sins" (1 John 4:10).

Paul had told the Philippians to "[stand] firm in one spirit" (1:27) and "[Be] of the same mind, maintaining the same love, united in spirit, intent on one purpose" (2:2). A believer's attitude toward another believer is tremendously important as they serve Christ together. It is not always easy for a Christian to have the right attitude toward another Christian. Paul did not indicate that it was easy, but by stating what the Lord Jesus Christ gave up in order to pay the penalty for sin, he thereby indicated that if Christians have the same attitude as Christ did, they will be able to live together harmoniously.

Chapter 15 – Jesus Christ: Lord Over All

For this reason also, God highly exalted Him, and bestowed on Him the name which is above every name (2:9).

PAUL HAD JUST explained what Jesus Christ did, which demonstrated the ultimate in putting others first. He left the glory He had with the Father in order to take upon Himself a body of flesh and to die a horrible death. But this humiliation was not the end of the story! Because Jesus Christ was willing to do this, "God highly exalted Him." Because the Lord Jesus Christ loved mankind so much, He was willing to leave the highest glory for the lowest estate, but as a result God had exalted Him from the lowest estate to the highest glory. The high-priestly prayer of the Lord Jesus had been answered: "Now, Father, glorify Me together with Yourself, with the glory which I had with You before the world was" (John 17:5).

More than a title was referred to when Paul said that God had given Him a "name which is above every name." A name simply represents all that a person is, so all of Christ's attributes are included by this reference. The word "name" (*onoma*) denotes the character, fame and authority of the person involved. It also relates to one's dignity or rank. None is higher in rank than the Lord Jesus Christ, not even the Father Himself. Today, when it is common for groups to emphasize that Jesus Christ is less than the Father, it is well to remember that the Jews clearly understood the claims of Jesus that He was "equal with God" (John 5:18), and this was why they sought to kill Him.

When Jesus Christ was on earth (as well as now that He is in heaven), many not only refused to acknowledge Him as the God of the universe, but they also refused to recognize His honor and authority. But someday this will all be different. One of the reasons the Lord Jesus Christ has been so highly exalted is:

So that at the name of Jesus EVERY KNEE WILL BOW, of those who are in heaven and on earth and under the earth (2:10).

The day is coming when everyone will have to acknowledge that Jesus Christ is Lord over all. Romans 14:11 says, "AS I LIVE, SAYS THE LORD, EVERY KNEE SHALL BOW TO ME, AND EVERY TONGUE SHALL GIVE PRAISE TO GOD." Both Philippians 2:10 and Romans 14:11 are drawn from Isaiah 45:23: "I have sworn by Myself, The word has gone forth from My mouth in righteousness and will not turn back, that to Me every knee will bow, every tongue will swear allegiance."

No realm will be exempt from having to submit to the Lord Jesus Christ. All will acknowledge Him—"those who are in heaven and on earth and under the earth." All creatures of the universe are divided into three categories: those in heaven, those in earth and those under the earth. No creature is left out in this threefold division. All people—believers, unbelievers and all angels, holy and fallen—will have to acknowledge submission "at the name of Jesus."

Although "Jesus" was a given name to the Lord when He entered the human race, it especially emphasizes His provision of salvation for mankind. Before the Lord Jesus Christ was physically born into the human race, the angel of the Lord announced to Joseph, "[Mary] will bear a Son; and you shall call His name Jesus, for He will save His people from their sins" (Matt. 1:21).

In order to be the Savior of the world, Jesus Christ had to be fully God as well as fully man. Thus, the name "Jesus" represents both His deity and His humanity. Because He is God, He is Lord of all. Because He took on human flesh, He was able to die on the cross and pay the full penalty for sin, and even those who do not believe in Him as their personal Savior will have to eventually acknowledge who He is and what He has done.

And that every tongue will confess that Jesus Christ is Lord, to the glory of God the Father (2:11).

"Every tongue" includes all created beings; none will be excluded in having to acknowledge that Jesus Christ is Lord.

The title "Lord" to the Jewish mind meant Jehovah-God. All these who will bow will not be believers in Jesus Christ as personal Savior, but all will be forced to acknowledge that He is God.

The word "confess" literally means, "to speak the same thing." Thus, it has the meaning of "agree," or "admit." All must someday agree, or admit, that Jesus Christ is God, even though they have not trusted Him as Savior.

Such an acknowledgement that Jesus Christ is Lord, or God, is "to the glory of God the Father." This is the key to whatever God does—to reflect His glory. Even the humiliation and exaltation of Christ, with eventual agreement by all that Jesus Christ is Lord, results in bringing glory to God.

Chapter 16 – A Passion to Please Christ

So then, my beloved, just as you have always obeyed, not as in my presence only, but now much more in my absence, work out your salvation with fear and trembling (2:12).

THE WORDS "SO THEN" reveal that Paul was referring to what he had just written. He had urged the Philippian believers to put others first (v. 3), then he had explained how Christ put others first even to the extent of emptying Himself of the glory He had with the Father and dying on the cross (vv.5-8). As a result God had highly exalted Jesus Christ, and someday every person will acknowledge that Jesus Christ is Lord (vv.9-11). So then, or on the basis of these truths, Paul was telling the believers to work out their salvation.

Paul's fondness of the Philippian believers is seen in his expression "my beloved." Paul had first come to Philippi on his second missionary journey. There he and Silas were beaten and thrown into prison but were miraculously delivered (see Acts 16:19-29). A close bond of fellowship had developed between Paul and the Philippians, and even before they left the city, Paul and Silas comforted the believers (v. 40).

No doubt Paul often wondered about the welfare of the believers in Philippi after what happened to him and Silas. These Christians were dear to Paul so, he addressed them as "my beloved" (Phil. 2:12).

Paul was about to urge the Philippians to fulfill a request, and he prefaced it by saying, "as you have always obeyed, not as in my presence only, but now much more in my absence." When the veteran apostle was on the scene in Philippi, there was no reluctance to obey his instructions; now he was concerned more than ever that they be obedient to what he was about to say, although he was not there in person.

Notice what he exhorted them to do: "Work out your salvation with fear and trembling." In the Greek text the phrase "with fear and trembling" comes before the statement "work out your salvation." This indicates that Paul was emphasizing their attitude as they fulfilled his injunction. The phrase "with fear and trembling" is also found in 2 Corinthians 7:15, where it refers to the Corinthians who had received Titus "with fear and trembling."

Concerning the expression, Dr. J. Dwight Pentecost points out "the idea behind it is of a passion to please" (*The Joy of Living*, p. 88). Just as the Corinthians had a passion to please Titus in all that they did for him, so the believer should have a passion to please the Lord Jesus Christ in all he does.

Paul's main command for the believers at Philippi was "Work out your salvation with fear and trembling." Those who believe that salvation is acquired by works usually point to this verse as an evidence of the relationship between works and salvation. However, the verse is not referring to a working in order to acquire salvation; rather, it is a referring to a working that expresses salvation.

The Bible makes it clear that works have no part in acquiring salvation. Ephesians 2:8-9, says, "For by grace you have been saved through faith; and that not of yourselves, *it is* the gift of God; not as a result of works, so that no one may boast."

For those who believe, however, it is important that they express the salvation they have as a result of placing their faith in Christ as Savior. This is what Paul referred to when he told the Philippian believers: "Work out your salvation." They already possessed salvation, but Paul was concerned that they work it out through their lives by expressing it in the activities of daily life.

For it is God who is at work in you, both to will and to work for *His* good pleasure (2:13).

This verse serves as an explanation of verse 12. The reason the Philippian believers were to work out their salvation was that God was working in them. The word translated "work" means "to work effectually." God does an effective work in a believer's life "both to will and to work for His good pleasure."

Two of the most basic needs of an individual Christian are the ability to do the right thing and the desire to do the right thing. This verse reveals that God gives both. He works in the believer to produce the will, and He works in the believer to actually accomplish His good pleasure. Of course, the believer has to respond to the working of God in his life if he is going to express characteristics that glorify God. Since God was already at work in the lives of the Philippian believers, Paul was urging them to express the working of God in everyday living.

The last words of verse 13 are literally "for good pleasure." The word "His" was added by the translators of the New American Standard Bible because it seems evident that it is God's good pleasure that is referred to in this verse. And what is His good pleasure? It is what Paul expressed earlier in this chapter when he said, "Make my joy complete by being of the same mind, maintaining the same love, united in spirit, intent on one purpose. Do nothing from selfishness or empty conceit, but with humility of mind regard one another as more important than yourselves; do not merely look out for your own personal interests, but also for the interests of others" (vv. 2-4).

Chapter 17 – Believers: Radiant Lights Among Believers

Do all things without grumbling or disputing (2:14).

HAVING TOLD THE Philippian believers to work out, or express, the salvation that was in them with a passion to please the Lord Jesus Christ, Paul then spelled out how this could be done. If the unbelieveing world is to see the outworking of the already in-worked salvation, it is necessary that believers "do all things without grumbling or disputing."

Although this is a short verse, it provides a lifetime goal for the believer. The difficulty of this verse is not how to understand the English, or even the Greek, but how to put into practice what Paul gave as an imperative if the unbelieving world is to be attracted to the Lord Jesus Christ.

In the Greek New Testament, the word "all" (*panta*) stands first in the sentence and, therefore, is strongly emphasized. Believers would have no problem with doing many things, or perhaps most things, without grumbling or disputing, but Paul said that all things were to be done in this way. Nothing was excluded.

For further emphasis the word translated "do" (*poieō*) is in the Greek present tense, which emphasizes a practice or continually doing something. Not only are all things included but also all time. Paul emphasized that this was to be the believer's way of life—the way a Christian works out, or expresses, his salvation.

The believer is always to do something "without grumbling or disputing." The word translated "grumbling" means "complaining, muttering." The believer who is characterized by a complaining attitude is not properly expressing the salvation he possesses; therefore, he is not attracting unbelievers to Jesus Christ. As Paul wrote he probably had the Old Testament Israelites in mind as those who dishonored God by a complaining spirit. In fact, in 1 Corinthians 10:10, Paul used the verb form of this same Greek word in telling believers: "Nor grumble, as some of them [the Israelites] did, and were destroyed by the destroyer." Paul went on to say, "Now these things happened to them as an example, and they were written for our instruction, upon whom the ends of the ages have come" (v. 11).

The believer who grumbles, or complains, does not have the confidence he should have in God's ability to use everything in his life to bring about his good and God's glory (see Rom. 8:28). This does not mean that an individual should be content with a miserable situation, but he should recognize that God can use even such situations to conform him to the image of Christ (see v. 29).

If those persons who know Christ as Savior are to attract others to the Lord, they must not only learn to do all things without murmuring but also without disputing. The Greek word translated "disputing" (*dialogismos*) is the word from which "dialogue" is derived. The Greek word means "doubt, dispute, argument." It has to do with expressing one's opinions; thus, the resultant meaning of arguing or debating.

"Disputing" is the state that logically follows "grumbling." Both prevent the believer from being the kind of witness he ought to be.

Why is it so important to do everything without grumbling and disputing? Paul answered that question in the following verse:

So that you will prove yourselves to be blameless and innocent, children of God above reproach in the midst of a crooked and perverse generation, among whom you appear as lights in the world (2:15).

The words "you will" are literally "may become." They indicated that the Philippians had not yet reached this state but that Paul was concerned that they might soon come to this place. As believers express the salvation they possess, it is necessary for them to be "blameless," or "innocent," before the watching world. Unbelievers should not be able to point a finger of accusation at the believer. Of course, no believer is perfect, but each Christian has a responsibility to face up to the wrongs he has committed against others. If he does not admit these wrongs, he will have the finger of accusation pointed at him.

Believers are also to be "innocent." The original word referred to that which is "pure." The believer is not to have mixed motives in what he does; he is not to connive to get his own way.

Paul also wanted the Philippian believers to come to that place where they would be "above reproach," that is, "unblemished." Just as the lamb bought for a sacrifice in the Old Testament had to be unblemished, so, too, believers ought to be unblemished as they walk before an unbelieving world.

As Paul described the type of world to whom each believer is a witness, he called it a "crooked and perverse generation." Paul must have been thinking at this point about the Old Testament Israelites who failed to believe God and as a result became "a perverse and crooked generation" (Deut. 32:5).

The Greek word Paul used for "crooked" in Philippians 2:15 meant "unscrupulous, dishonest." This is the kind of world in which the believer lives and is to glorify Christ. The word "perverse" is translated from a word meaning "perverted, depraved." It is a combination of two Greek words, one meaning "to turn," with another word added which intensifies the meaning. The world has turned from the truth and, thus, has become perverted and depraved.

What Paul told the Philippian believers is true of every believer today: "among whom you appear as lights in the world." Notice that Paul did not command the believers to shine; rather, he stated that they were shining. Even the believer with a poor testimony shines before an unbelieving world, but Paul was concerned that each believer have a good witness before the world. A good witness would stand in even greater contrast to the unscrupulous and perverted. Believers shine radiantly before the world as they "do all things without grumbling or disputing" (v. 14). Those who do things without grumbling or disputing are "blameless and innocent" and "above reproach" (v. 15).

Holding fast the word of life, so that in the day of Christ I will have reason to glory because I did not run in vain nor toil in vain (2:16).

The words "holding fast" seem to have two possible meanings. One view is that they involve the idea of "holding out" as one would offer food or a gift to someone. This fits the analogy of the believer's walking in an unbelieving world, holding out the Word of God to all who will believe. Another possibility is that the words fit the analogy of the believer's need to hold fast to the Word of Life as he seeks to be a radiant testimony in a crooked and perverse world.

Although either meaning of these words fits the context, uses of the same Greek word (*epechō*) elsewhere in the New Testament seem to support more the idea of "holding fast." The same word is used in Acts 19:22 where it is said that Paul "stayed [*epechō*] in Asia." Paul retained his position rather than going to another place. He held fast where he was.

The Greek word translated "holding fast" in Philippians 2:16 is a present active participle, which indicates the action goes on at the same time as the action of the main verb. That is, the Philippian believers were shining as lights in the world while holding fast to the Word of Life.

This shows the centrality of the Word of God to the believer's witness. The Christian is to study the Word, apply it to himself and then translate it into daily living before a crooked and perverse world.

Paul expressed why he was concerned that the Philippian believers be effective witnesses while holding fast to the Word of Life: "I will have reason to glory because I did not run in vain nor toil in vain." Paul was concerned that, on the day when all believers give an account to Jesus Christ for the way they have served Him in this life, the believers from Philippi would receive rewards. This would be proof to Paul that his ministry with them had not been in vain, or empty. Here one sees the concern of the veteran apostle for those he had discipled in the faith. For them to be radiant witnesses while clinging to the Word of God would cause him to rejoice in the day when every believer gives account to the Lord Jesus Christ.

Chapter 18 - Content to Pour Out His Life

HAVING EXPRESSED HIS desire to rejoice in the Day of Christ that he had not labored in vain for the Philippians, Paul said:

But even if I am being poured out as a drink offering upon the sacrifice and service of your faith, I rejoice and share my joy with you all (2:17).

Even as he wrote, the Apostle Paul realized that he might be called on to give his life for the cause of Christ. The word he used for "offering" is *spendō*, which was used of a drink offering poured out as a libation, or sacrifice, to God. Paul had suffered much for the cause of Christ. Even at this time, he was imprisoned in Rome, but he had no regrets if he had to give his life for the sake of the gospel. In fact, he looked at such a privilege as an act of worshipping God—being poured out as a drink offering.

In the last letter we have from his pen, Paul used the same Greek word when he said, "For I am already being poured [*spendō*] out as a drink offering, and the time of my departure has come" (2 Tim. 4:6). Shortly after writing 2 Timothy, history indicates that Paul gave his life for the gospel, although the Scriptures do not record his death.

Paul was not one to view his physical death as a defeat. Elsewhere he said, "We are of good courage, I say, and prefer…to be absent from the body and to be at home with the Lord" (2 Cor. 5:8). Earlier in his letter to the Philippians, he had written: "For to me, to live is Christ and to die is gain" (1:21). So as he wrote concerning offering himself upon the sacrifice and service of the Philippians' faith, we can be sure that he was not feeling sorry for himself. Quite the opposite was true; he said, "I rejoice and share my joy with you all" (2:17).

Notice how Paul viewed himself as being poured out as a drink offering for the Philippians: "But even if I am being poured out as a drink offering upon the sacrifice and service of your faith" (v. 17). As the Philippians expressed their faith, they produced what amounted to a sacrifice and service to God.

The Greek word Paul used for "sacrifice" (*thusia*) was the same word he used when he told believers in Rome, "Present your bodies a living and holy sacrifice, acceptable to God" (Rom. 12:1). This was strange terminology for those in the first century who knew about sacrifices to the pagan gods as well as the Jewish sacrifices to the true God. A sacrifice is dead, yet Paul told the Roman believers to present their bodies "a living and holy sacrifice."

God does call upon some believers to give their lives for Him, as He did the Apostle Paul, most of the other apostles and many others throughout church history. But the normal demand that God makes of a believer is that his entire life be a "living" sacrifice. If God calls upon believers who know Him as Savior to give their lives for Him, they can be sure that He will give them the special grace needed at such a time. But the believers concern should be that they live in such a way that their lives serve as an act of worship of God.

Not only were the good works of the Philippians viewed as a sacrifice, but they were also used as a "service" (2:17). The Greek word translated "service" was *leitourgia* and was commonly used of serving God. This word is translated "ministry" in Hebrews 9:21, which states concerning Moses: "He sprinkled both the tabernacle and all the vessels of the ministry with the blood." Thus, the "service" of the Philippians was considered an act of worship of God.

Again, notice that Paul did not bemoan the fact that he might be called upon to pour out his life as a sacrifice and service for the Philippians. Instead, he said that if this were the case: "I rejoice and share my joy with you all" (2:17). What a tremendous example Paul is of one who had victory over circumstances! He had every reason to feel sorry for himself, but he refused to do so. Instead of despairing and complaining, he was rejoicing!

No doubt the Philippian believers had been saddened by Paul's imprisonment and were deeply concerned about him. Think of the response they must have had when they read the letter and learned that he was rejoicing. No doubt this gave them mixed emotions, but as they read on, they would see that Paul was demanding something of them in this regard.

You too, *I urge you*, rejoice in the same way and share your joy with me (2:18).

Paul was not content to merely have personal victory over circumstances; he wanted fellow believers to share in his victory. Instead of allowing the Philippians to sorrow over the possibility that Paul might have to give his life for the preaching of the gospel, he wanted them to rejoice that God had given him the privilege of pouring out his life as a drink offering.

Paul was certainly convinced that the death of a believer glorifies God. When Jesus predicted what kind of death Peter would die, the Apostle John stated in his Gospel: "Signifying by what kind of death he would glorify God" (21:19). Although the believer dies physically, he goes immediately to be in the presence of the Lord. So, in a sense, he is more alive than he has ever been! Death entered the world because of sin (Rom. 5:12), yet even as a believer experiences death, he has the distinct privilege of bringing glory to God. It is not evident from the Scriptures precisely how a believer brings glory to God in his death. But it is clear that from God's viewpoint a believer's death is a time of triumph rather than defeat.

The Lord Jesus Christ shed His blood on the cross so that all who believe in Him as Savior could be delivered from condemnation and could someday dwell in His presence. Although his body goes to the grave at the time of physical death, the believer goes directly to be with the Lord, which is the fulfillment of what Christ came to do for fallen mankind.

Chapter 19 – Paul Sends a Like-minded Missionary

But I hope in the Lord Jesus to send Timothy to you shortly, so that I also may be encouraged when I learn of your condition (2:19).

PAUL DESPERATELY WANTED to know how the Philippian believers were progressing in their spiritual lives. Because he was in prison and unable to go to them personally, Paul decided to send Timothy to visit them and to bring back a report. Timothy was well acquainted with the believers in Philippi, for he was with Paul on the second missionary journey when Paul and Silas were imprisoned in Philippi (see Acts 16).

At the time Paul wrote, he did not expect to wait long before sending Timothy to check on the Philippians. Paul was uneasy as he wondered about the Philippians' spiritual progress, and he planned to send Timothy to them soon to bring back a report and put his mind at ease.

This gives us an insight into the life of the Apostle Paul. He was concerned about the progress of new Christians. They were on his mind even though he himself was in a trial before the Roman court. Paul did not enter an area, proclaim the gospel, count converts and then leave without thinking of the people again. The main purpose of Paul's second missionary journey was to revisit the areas where he had been to see how the new Christians were doing (see Acts 15:36). So, it was consistent with the Apostle Paul's life that he wanted to learn more information about the Philippian believers so he could be at ease concerning them.

The fact that Paul had decided to send Timothy to Philippi was highly significant. Timothy had been one of Paul's closest companions, but Paul had decided to send him anyway. Since Paul was in prison at the time, this was an unselfish decision, for Paul surely craved the fellowship that Timothy could provide. But Paul saw no alternative but to send Timothy. Paul said:

For I have no one else of kindred spirit who will genuinely be concerned for your welfare (2:20).

The Greek word translated "kindred" is *isopsuchos*, meaning "of like soul" or "of like mind." The *iso* part of this word has the sense of "equal to." There was no one else equal to Timothy that Paul could send to Philippi to check on the believers there. Since no one else was as qualified as Timothy, Paul chose to be without his close companion for a time in order to learn about the Philippians.

Paul had no one like Timothy who would naturally care about the Philippians. The word translated "genuinely" is *gnēsiōs*, meaning "sincerely." This is the only time this Greek word occurs in the New Testament. Timothy's quality of soul was such that he genuinely cared for the Philippian believers, and Paul knew of no one else who qualified like Timothy to be sent to Philippi.

The reason Paul gave was a sad commentary on the others:

For they all seek after their own interests, not those of Christ Jesus (2:21).

Concerning this verse, commentators are usually quick to point out that Paul could not have been referring to such people as Luke, who had faithfully served him. This statement applied to Christians in general and especially to any Paul might have wanted to send to Philippi instead of Timothy. Rather than seeking that which furthered the cause of Jesus Christ, they were guilty of seeking things which furthered their own cause. In a word, they were selfish.

Some in the church in Corinth were also selfish, and Paul referred to them as "fleshly." He wrote: "And I, brethren, could not speak to you as to spiritual men, but as to men of flesh, as to infants in Christ. For you are still fleshly. For since there is jealousy and strife among you, are you not fleshly, and are you not walking like mere men?" (1 Cor. 3:1,3). Wherever there is envying, strife, and divisions, it is evident that Christians are seeking their own interests rather than the interests of Christ.

But Timothy stood in great contrast to those other Christians; he put the things of Christ before his own interests. With such quality of soul, no wonder Paul willingly invested his life in discipling Timothy.

Chapter 20 – Paul Sends His Trusted Servant

But you know of his proven worth, that he served with me in the furtherance of the gospel like a child *serving* his father (2:22).

IN THIS VERSE Paul referred to Timothy, whom he planned to send to the Philippians (v. 19). Paul had no choice but to send Timothy because no one else cared enough about the Philippians (v. 20). Others were too involved in their own interests to make a trip to Philippi to learn how it was going with the believers there (v. 21).

Having mentioned that he would soon send Timothy, Paul went on to refer to Timothy's qualities. In contrast to those who were too involved in their own interests to be sent to Philippi, Paul said, "But you know of his proven worth" (v. 22). The Philippian believers had had opportunity to observe Timothy closely, so they knew from experience what he was like.

The word translated "proven" is *dokimē*, which refers to that which has the quality of being approved. This word was commonly used of the testing of metals and coins. It could refer either to the process of the testing itself or to the result of the testing, which was approval. It is the result of testing that Paul had in mind in this context because the Philippians had viewed Timothy's testing and knew his approved condition because of the testing.

Testing accomplishes something in one's life that allows him to be better used in the future. Had it not been for the testing through which Timothy had gone, his value to Paul at this time would not have been as great. He was a trusted servant as well as a precious fellow Christian. Paul was relying on him to go soon to the Philippians to learn about them and bring back a report.

Involved in Timothy's proving himself was that he had served with Paul "like a child *serving* his father." The word Paul used for "child" was *teknon*, which was commonly used of a child, in contrast to *huios*, which referred to a son's full-fledged position in the family. Paul viewed Timothy as a child who worked not only *for* his father but also *with* him.

It is evident that Paul looked on Timothy as a spiritual son. There is no direct evidence in the Scriptures that Paul had actually led Timothy to the Lord, but at least he had had the major responsibility in discipling Timothy. The words "my true child" (1 Tim. 1:2) and "my beloved son" (2 Tim. 1:2) have often been used to suggest that Paul led Timothy to the Lord. However, there is no support in the Greek text for the word "my" in either of these verses. The first expression should literally read "a genuine child," and the second literally reads "a beloved child." Since Paul had such a close relationship in discipling Timothy, however, it was understandable that Paul looked on him as a son.

Timothy had served with Paul "in the furtherance of the gospel" (Phil. 2:22). The word Paul used for "in" was *eis*. In this construction, the word has the sense of "with a view to." All that Timothy and Paul had done together had been with the gospel in view. In the interest of the gospel, Timothy had served Paul faithfully, which was Timothy's way of serving God faithfully. The Philippians would have been well aware that Timothy's motivation for service was his interest in furthering the gospel of the Lord Jesus Christ.

Having stressed Timothy's qualifications, Paul said:

Therefore I hope to send him immediately, as soon as I see how things *go* with me (2:23).

Paul here emphasized that this one he had been describing was the very one he would send to the Philippians. Not just any representative of Paul's would be paying them a visit. Surely the Philippians were thrilled to hear this news. It was the next best thing to being visited by Paul himself!

Paul repeated that he hoped to send Timothy soon. In verse 19, Paul had stated: "I hope in the Lord Jesus to send Timothy to you shortly." Now he wrote: "Therefore I hope to send him immediately." Paul did not want to leave any doubt about his concern for the Philippians, so he stressed that Timothy would come as soon as possible.

However, Timothy was to wait for one thing before beginning his trip to Philippi. He was to wait for the news of the outcome of Paul's trial. Paul promised to send Timothy "as soon as I see how things *go* with me." The Philippians would not be left wondering about the outcome of Paul's trial. As soon as the decision was reached, Timothy was to be sent to them. Then they would know how Paul was faring, and he would be able to learn how the Philippians were doing. Paul, writing these words from his Roman prison, apparently expected to learn the outcome of his trial soon.

It is evident what Paul expected the outcome of the trial to be, for he told the Philippians:

And I trust in the Lord that I myself also will be coming shortly (2:24).

The word translated "trust" is *peithō*, which means "to convince" or "to persuade." The word is used in the Greek perfect tense, emphasizing something that had taken place in the past with a continuing effect. In other words, Paul had been persuaded in the past—and still was convinced at the time of writing—that he was going to be released from prison and would be able to visit the Philippians shortly. He had confidence that the Lord was going to work things out so he would be released and would have the joy of being with these believers again.

It may have taken longer than Paul thought for the trial to culminate, but the indication is that he was eventually released from prison. It was later, during his second imprisonment in Rome that he wrote 2 Timothy, the last letter we have from his pen.

These verses in Philippians show Paul's great concern for those he had evangelized earlier. He wanted to know that they were progressing in the things of the Lord because this is what brought joy to him. It serves as an important lesson for believers today not only to be concerned about evangelizing and leading others to Christ but also to be diligent in follow-up to encourage spiritual growth.

Chapter 21 –
Epaphroditus: Paul's
Link With Philippi

But I thought it necessary to send to you Epaphroditus, my brother and fellow worker and fellow soldier, who is also your messenger and minister to my need (2:25).

EPAPHRODITUS IS MENTIONED by name only twice in Philippians—here and in 4:18. In the latter verse Paul said, "But I have received everything in full and have an abundance; I am amply supplied, having received from Epaphroditus what you have sent, a fragrant aroma, an acceptable sacrifice, well-pleasing to God."

A shortened form of the name was Epaphras, although Epaphroditus of Philippians 2:25 and 4:18 is generally considered to be a different person than the Epaphras mentioned in Colossians 1:7 and 4:12 and in Philemon 1:23.

Paul indicated by his statement in Philippians 4:18 that the Philippians had earlier sent Epaphroditus to Rome, bearing gifts for Paul from the church. No doubt the church at Philippi intended for Epaphroditus to be whatever help he could be to the apostle during Paul's trial. But as Paul wrote to the Philippians, he said, "But I thought it necessary to send to you Epaphroditus" (2:25). Even though the Philippians had sent Epaphroditus earlier to Paul, the apostle was actually sending Epaphroditus back to them.

Notice that Paul used the past tense, as indicated by the

word translated "thought." It was a custom in New Testament times to write a letter from the standpoint of the reader rather than from the standpoint of the writer. For instance, by the time the Philippians read Paul's letter Epaphroditus already would have returned to the church. Although Paul was expressing his present desires at the time he was writing, Epaphroditus's return would have been an accomplished fact when the letter arrived—thus the past tense from the readers' standpoint.

It is especially interesting to notice the way in which Paul referred to Epaphroditus: "my brother and fellow worker and fellow soldier." Each of these terms refers to a different aspect. "Brother" emphasized the affection Paul had for Epaphroditus and the oneness he felt with him. "Fellow worker" emphasized their oneness in sharing a common burden. Both of them desired to further the cause of Christ. Paul accomplished this by proclaiming the gospel to the Gentiles, whereas Epaphroditus's way was by being a servant—at this time a servant to the Apostle Paul. It is significant that Paul did not elevate himself above Epaphroditus, even though their responsibilities were significantly different—one in the limelight and the other behind the scenes.

"Fellow soldier" emphasized that both Paul and Epaphroditus were engaged in spiritual warfare. Paul was fond of using military terminology as an analogy to the Christian life, such as in Ephesians 6:11-17 and 2 Timothy 2:3-4. He was intensely aware that Christians battle against the world, flesh and the Devil. Recognizing his victorious position in Christ, Paul fought the spiritual battle successfully. At the end of his life he was able to say, "I have fought the good fight, I have finished the course, I have kept the faith" (2 Tim. 4:7).

Although Epaphroditus was Paul's brother, fellow worker and fellow soldier, he was a messenger of the Philippians.

Paul said, "Who is also your messenger and minister to my need" (2:25). Epaphroditus had been officially sent by the Philippians and had ministered to Paul during his Roman imprisonment.

Paul then told the Philippians why he was sending Epaphroditus back to them:

Because he was longing for you all and was distressed because you had heard that he was sick (2:26).

The burden Epaphroditus held for the Philippians is indicated by the words translated "longing" and "distressed." The word *epipotheō* is an intense word for longing or desire. The word translated "distressed" is a form of *adēmoneō*, meaning, "be anxious." An example of this word used in secular writing of that time has been translated "excessively concerned" (*The Vocabulary of the Greek New Testament*, p. 9). So it was more than Epaphroditus being concerned about the Philippians; he was intensely burdened for them.

Why was he so burdened for them? Paul gave the answer: "Because you had heard that he was sick" (v. 26). Apparently, Epaphroditus was so concerned, after he learned that the Philippians knew he had been sick, because he felt so badly that they had sent him as their messenger and yet he had not been able to fulfill his tasks. In addition, he had been a burden to the Philippians because they were so concerned about him. And their concern was justified. Paul explained:

For indeed he was sick to the point of death, but God had mercy on him, and not on him only but also on me, so that I would not have sorrow upon sorrow (2:27).

Epaphroditus was so ill that he nearly died. In the light of the emphasis today in some theological circles on miraculous healing, it is interesting to observe that Epaphroditus was in the presence of the Apostle Paul, and yet there is no indication that Paul did anything miraculous on his behalf. To the contrary, Paul indicated that it was God who had mercy on both Epaphroditus and him. Although Epaphroditus was at the point of death, and there was apparently no human hope for him, God spared him. This greatly encouraged Paul. If Epaphroditus would have died, in addition to Paul's problems of imprisonment, he would have experienced sorrow for this one who had been a "brother" (v. 25). This would have been "sorrow upon sorrow" (v. 27) for the apostle.

Observe that apparently even the Apostle Paul experienced sorrow when a fellow believer died, even though he knew such a person was going immediately into the presence of the Lord. Paul said elsewhere, "We are of good courage, I say, and prefer rather to be absent from the body and to be at home with the Lord" (2 Cor. 5:8). But although Paul sorrowed for fellow believers who died, he did not sorrow as those who have no hope (see 1 Thess. 4:13). So we see that this passage from Philippians gives insight not only into the life of Epaphroditus but also into the life of the Apostle Paul.

Chapter 22 –
Epaphroditus:
Deserving of Honor

Therefore I have sent him all the more eagerly so that when you see him again you may rejoice and I may be less concerned *about you* **(2:28).**

THE APOSTLE PAUL here referred to Epaphroditus, whom the Philippians had sent to Paul as their messenger and representative to minister to his needs (v. 25). Epaphroditus had assisted Paul during his Roman imprisonment but had become ill in the process. The Philippian believers heard about his sickness and were greatly burdened about it, not only because he was not able to minister adequately to Paul but also because they felt empathy for this servant of God. Apparently they felt as bad about his being sick as they would have been concerning their own sickness.

So in writing to the Philippian believers, Paul said, "I have sent him all the more eagerly" (v. 28). The words "more eagerly" are a translation of *spoudaiōs*, which means "with haste" or "with special urgency." Paul was returning Epaphroditus to the Philippian believers more quickly than he otherwise would have. If Epaphroditus had been in good health and the Philippians had not been so concerned about him, there would have been no need to send him so hastily to them. Also, Epaphroditus desperately wanted to return to Philippi (v. 26). So for the good of both the Philippians and Epaphroditus, Paul was hastily sending him to them.

Paul anticipated what their response would be at seeing Epaphroditus: "That when you see him again you may rejoice" (v. 28). Paul knew the Philippian believers would be delighted when they saw Epaphroditus. This gives an insight into the concern the Philippians had for the representative they had sent to take care of Paul's needs.

Paul added, "And I may be less concerned *about you*" (v. 28). The apostle's statement indicates that he would also be relieved to know that Epaphroditus was back with the Philippians. Even though Paul had greatly appreciated what Epaphroditus had done for him, he was exceedingly concerned about his condition. Therefore, it was undoubtedly a relief for Paul to anticipate Epaphroditus being back home where he would be properly cared for. Paul then instructed the Philippians to welcome Epaphroditus:

Receive him then in the Lord with all joy, and hold men like him in high regard (2:29).

The word "receive" is from the basic form *dechomai* which has the emphasis of "welcome" in it. This was the same word Luke used in referring to the Bereans who "received the word with great eagerness, examining the Scriptures daily *to see* whether these things were so" (Acts 17:11).

Thus, Paul wanted the Philippians to welcome Epaphroditus "with all joy" (Phil. 2:29). Paul did not want the Philippians to hold back any expression of joy as they welcomed Epaphroditus home.

Paul also enjoined them to "hold men like him in high regard" (v. 29). Apparently Epaphroditus was not noted among the believers in Philippi as a gifted teacher or leader, but Paul wanted him to be welcomed home with the highest honor. He had been able to help Paul in ways that a gifted teacher or leader may not have been able to, and Paul was deeply grateful for all that had been done.

Paul explained why high honor should be given to Epaphroditus:

Because he came close to death for the work of Christ, risking his life to complete what was deficient in your service to me (2:30).

Paul viewed Epaphroditus's sickness to be directly related to the "work of Christ." Many believers during Paul's time had suffered persecution for the cause of Christ and had earned the praise of other believers. Because of Epaphroditus's illness, Paul believed he was deserving of honor in the Body of Christ. Although Paul does not give details, apparently this illness was directly related to Epaphroditus coming to Rome to minister to Paul's needs.

Paul gave insight into Epaphroditus's dedication when he said of him, "Risking his life." This phrase can be literally translated "having gambled with his life." The indication is that Epaphroditus had known ahead of time the risk he was taking in coming to Rome, but he willingly did so to be of help to the Apostle Paul and, in a broader sense, to further the work of Christ. No wonder Paul had wanted the Philippian believers to welcome Epaphroditus home with joy and to hold him in high honor.

Paul told the Philippians that the reason Epaphroditus had risked his life was "to complete what was deficient in your service to me" (v. 30). Since Epaphroditus had been sent as their representative, the intent of Paul's words seems to be that Epaphroditus did what the Philippians would have liked, but were unable, to do. Because they could not personally come to Paul's aid, they had sent Epaphroditus as their special representative.

With these concluding remarks about Epaphroditus, Paul brought to a close this section of his letter to the Philippians which stresses the importance of having the mind of Christ and of putting others first. Paul had urged them to think in this way and then told of individuals who had done so. After referring to the Lord Jesus Christ, who gave up all for the sake of others, Paul also mentioned himself, Timothy and Epaphroditus as examples of those who put others first. Surely none could have read the letter at the time without getting Paul's point. And surely no believer today can read this chapter without getting Paul's point. And surely no believer today can read this chapter without seeing the importance of thinking as Christ thought, which results in putting others first.

Chapter 23 – "It is a Safeguard For You."

Finally, my brethren, rejoice in the Lord. To write the same things again is no trouble to me, and it is a safeguard for you (3:1).

ALTHOUGH "FINALLY" IS an acceptable translation for *loipon*, in this context it can have other shades of meaning. The word also has the sense of "the remaining" or "the rest." The same word appears in 4:8 and is also translated "finally" in the New American Standard Version.

In 3:1 Paul likely used *loipon* simply to indicate that he was about to touch on another subject. It is also possible that Paul was about to conclude the epistle but first wanted to inject something of extreme importance before he did so.

Addressing the Philippian believers as "brethren" (3:1), Paul told them to "rejoice in the Lord." The word translated "rejoice" (*chairō*) is a familiar word to the Philippians. It occurs in 1:18; 2:17, 18, 28; 3:1; 4:4,10. The New American Standard Version translates it "rejoice" each time.

This is a key word in Philippians, even though Paul was writing from prison at the time. Paul was at least under guard and was possibly in chains while he kept emphasizing to the Philippian believers the importance of rejoicing. Not only is rejoicing emphasized in Philippians by the number of times the word occurs, but also in 3:1 Paul used the word in the present tense, which emphasizes continuous action. He wanted the Philippian believers to keep on rejoicing.

Notice, however, the sphere in which Paul wanted the believers to rejoice—"in the Lord." Paul was not able to rejoice in his circumstances at the time, and he realized that the Philippian believers may not have been able to do so either, but they could rejoice in the Lord. In spite of their circumstances, each one who had trusted Jesus Christ as personal Savior had a perfect position in Christ, and such a realization brought joy far deeper than circumstances ever could.

Paul told the Philippian believers: "To write the same things again is no trouble to me, and it is a safeguard for you." A question arises as to what Paul referred to by "the same things." Perhaps he referred to something already mentioned in this letter, or perhaps he referred to other letters he had written to them since he had left Philippi. Since there seems to be little in the first part of the letter that parallels what he is about to say, he was apparently referring to warnings he had given them earlier.

Sometimes preachers are hesitant to tell their people the same things, but Paul never hesitated to do this when necessary. He had apparently warned them earlier about false teachers, commonly known as "Judaizers," and he was going to do so again.

To remind them of these same things, he said, was "no trouble to me." The word Paul used for "trouble" (*oknēros*) referred to something "troublesome." The word can also mean "lazy." Paul was emphasizing that it was not lazy of him to repeat what he had told them before because it was evident they needed to be warned again. It is interesting to observe that Paul thought repetition would bring the charge of laziness against him because he emphasized that this was not the case.

Instead of a repeated warning being the indication of laziness, it was motivated by his concern for their safety—

"and it is a safeguard for you" (3:1). He was concerned about their spiritual safety. The following verse contains his serious warning:

Beware of the dogs, beware of the evil workers, beware of the false circumcision (3:2).

Each warning is prefaced by the word "beware," which was the common word meaning "to see." In this context it means to "watch" or to "beware of."

Paul wanted the Philippian believers to watch out for "dogs." Because there are so many pet dogs in the western world the full force of Paul's statement is not usually evident. In the Middle East during Paul's time, dogs were normally ownerless scavengers—about as unclean an animal as one could find. The Jews had commonly referred to the uncleanness of the Gentiles by calling them "dogs," but Paul turned it around and used the term to refer to Jews who were confused about the gospel. They were mixing works with the gospel of grace, so although those Jews claimed to be the clean ones, they were in reality the spiritually unclean ones.

Paul also told the Philippian believers to watch out for "evil workers." Instead of seeing the Judaizers as doers of good that would bring glory to God, Paul viewed them as evil workers because they were reducing the Christian life to a system of do's and don'ts.

Paul also warned, "Beware of the false circumcision" (v. 2). The word "circumcision" (*katatomē*) means "mutilation." The Jews were concerned about circumcision because this was a sign of God's covenant with Abraham (see Gen. 17:11). Many of the Jews during Paul's day had trusted Jesus Christ as Savior, but some were confusing the gospel of grace by teaching that circumcision was required for salvation. Paul viewed circumcision as simply mutilation if it were taught as being essential to salvation.

By extension, similar things can be said about anything else that would be added to the gospel of salvation, which is by grace alone. Church membership, confirmation, water baptism—good works or anything that is added to the gospel of grace corrupts the teaching concerning salvation. Paul's simple command to the jailer in Philippi, as well as to his household, was "Believe in the Lord Jesus, and you will be saved" (Acts 16:31).

After a person has placed his trust in Jesus Christ as his personal Savior, there are many things he should do to express that salvation. But those things are not required for salvation; rather, they are the result of it.

Most of the Philippian believers were Gentiles. Yet Paul told them:

For we are the *true* circumcision, who worship in the Spirit of God and glory in Christ Jesus and put no confidence in the flesh (3:3).

Since Paul was writing to Gentiles, he was not referring to physical circumcision but to a spiritual circumcision. But even in the Old Testament times physical circumcision was intended to point to the circumcision of the heart. Moses told the Israelites, "The Lord your God will circumcise your heart and the heart of your descendants, to love the Lord your God with all your heart and with all your soul, so that you may live" (Deut. 30:6).

Many of the Jews during Paul's time, however, were emphasizing only the importance of physical circumcision without any emphasis on the importance of the circumcision of the heart, or spiritual circumcision. Because Paul was writing to believers, he told the Philippians: "We are the true circumcision" (Phil. 3:3). The meaning of true circumcision is revealed by Paul's following statements: "Who worship in the Spirit of God and glory in Christ Jesus and put no confidence in the flesh."

The sect in Paul's time known as the Pharisees centered almost its entire attention on that which was physical rather than on that which was spiritual. The group was more concerned about do's and don'ts than about personal righteousness. Paul let it be known that those who are in right relationship to Jesus Christ live on a far higher plane, for they worship God "in the Spirit." The preposition translated "in" can also be translated "by." The believer worships God by means of the indwelling Holy Spirit.

Believers are also those who "glory in Christ Jesus." The word translated "glory" is not the common one used throughout Philippians, but instead it is a word meaning "to boast." Rather than boasting or having confidence in the flesh—as the Judaizers did—believers are those who boast in what they have in Jesus Christ.

Paul was not indicating that a believer should be unconcerned about how he lives, but he was stressing that the Christian life, which results from a personal relationship with Jesus Christ, is not to be reduced to a mere system of do's and don'ts.

Chapter 24 –
"Confidence in the
Flesh" – Worthless

**Although I myself might have confidence even in the flesh.
If anyone else has a mind to put confidence in the flesh, I
far more (3:4).**

AS PAUL WROTE to the believers in Philippi to warn them
about the Judaizers, he forcefully argued against the basic
element in Judaism—confidence in the flesh. Those who were
still living by the system of the Old Testament Law judged
another's relationship to God on the basis of the flesh. This
would include not only a person's physical lineage but also
whether or not he had been circumcised as the Mosaic Law
specified.

As Paul endeavored to show that the believer in Christ has
no confidence in the flesh (Phil. 3:3), he chose first of all to
revel that he, more than anyone else, might have confidence in
the flesh.

Paul said, "If anyone else has a mind to put confidence in
the flesh, I far more" (3:4). Apparently it was commonly
known among the Jews of his day that none had excelled to
the extent Paul had. Concerning his life before trusting in
Christ, he had told the Galatian believers, "I was advancing in
Judaism beyond many of my contemporaries among my

countrymen, being more extremely zealous for my ancestral traditions" (Gal. 1:14).

So as Paul spoke out against the heresies of Judaism as he wrote to the Philippians, he listed his qualifications, which would show anyone who wanted to boast in accomplishments that he had more reason to boast than anyone else.

Circumcised the eighth day, of the nation of Israel, of the tribe of Benjamin, a Hebrew of Hebrews; as to the Law, a Pharisee (3:5).

Paul began his list by citing the item that the Judaizers were most concerned about—circumcision. Paul was able to see that he was circumcised on the eighth day, which was in strict observance of the Mosaic Law (see Lev. 12:3). Probably many of the Judaizers could not have boasted about this, for some were no doubt Gentiles who had converted to Judaism and had been circumcised as adults. For any who thought that circumcision was essential to salvation, Paul made it clear that this amounted to turning circumcision into "false circumcision" (Phil. 3:2), that is, a mutilating of the flesh.

Paul went on to state: "of the nation of Israel" (v. 5). He did not have a mixed parentage as would have been true of some of the Judaizers. Paul could trace his lineage to Abraham, Isaac and Jacob, whose name was changed to "Israel" (Gen. 32:28).

Paul added another qualification: "of the tribe of Benjamin" (Phil. 3:5). Not only could Paul claim to be an Israelite, but he could also prove to which tribe he belonged. Some were not able to do that because some of the genealogical records had been lost or destroyed during the Babylonian captivity after the temple was destroyed in 586 B.C. Israel's first king (Saul) came from the tribe of Benjamin (see 1 Sam. 9:1,2).

Paul added: "a Hebrew of Hebrews" (Phil. 3:5). Some of the Israelites had adopted the Greek Language and Greek customs, but Paul was "a Hebrew of the Hebrews" because he knew the Hebrew customs and spoke the Hebrew language. None could put himself above Paul in this regard.

"As to the Law, a Pharisee" (v. 5). The Pharisees were the strictest sect of Judaism. They not only paid careful attention to the Mosaic Law but also added many regulations of their own. Some of the theological differences between the Pharisees and the Sadducees (another prominent sect) are recorded in Acts 23:8: "For the Sadducees say that there is no resurrection, nor an angel, nor a spirit, but the Pharisees acknowledge them all." Since Paul was a Pharisee, he had much to boast about according to the flesh as far as Judaism was concerned.

As to zeal, a persecutor of the church; as to righteousness which is in the Law, found blameless (3:6).

The Jews were particularly fanatical against those who claimed that Jesus Christ was the Messiah. Paul indicated he had evidenced more zeal than his countrymen in this regard because he persecuted the church.

In fact, this was the reason he was on his way to Damascus when he was struck down by the Lord and placed his faith in Jesus Christ as his Savior. Acts 9:1-2 says, "Now Saul, still breathing threats and murder against the disciples of the Lord, went to the high priest, and asked for letters from him to the synagogues at Damascus, so that if he found any belonging to the Way, both men and women, he might bring them bound to Jerusalem." No Judaizer could boast of more zeal directed against the Christians than could Paul.

Because the Judaizers were boasting in the Law, Paul said, "as to righteousness which is in the Law, found blameless" (Phil. 3:6). Paul was so zealous in the Jewish religion before his conversion to Jesus Christ that he had met all the requirements of the Law. Surely this was something that not all Judaizers could have claimed.

If salvation was based on a person's birth into the right family or on keeping the Law or on zeal, Paul had nothing to worry about. But in the following verses Paul went on to reveal that all he had done in his sincerity was worthless as far as coming into right relationship with God was concerned. Thus, Paul serves as a key example that salvation is not obtained by the things a person does or by his sincerity but only by placing faith in Jesus Christ as one's personal Savior.

Chapter 25 - The Gain Was Really Loss

But whatever things were gain to me, those things I have counted as loss for the sake of Christ (3:7).

THE JUDAIZERS WERE troubling and confusing the Philippian believers, and Paul was endeavoring to set these matters straight. The Judaizers taught that it was necessary to keep the regulations of the Mosaic Law in order to be right with God and to mature spiritually. Because of the emphasis on the Mosaic Law there was also an emphasis on what a person had accomplished in this life.

Paul was explaining to the Philippian believers that he, more than anyone else, had the right to boast because of what he had accomplished in the Jewish religion (vv. 5-6). Paul's list would have been admired by any of the Judaizers then troubling the Philippian believers. But after itemizing his accomplishments according to the flesh, Paul said, "But whatever things were gain to me, those things I have counted as loss for the sake of Christ" (v. 7). Paul used the Greek word for gain (*kerdos*) in its plural form, thereby stressing the many gains he had accomplished according to the standards of the Judaizers. But notice what Paul said about those gains.

"Those things I have counted as loss for the sake of Christ" (v. 7). The word translated "counted" (*hēgeomai*) means "to think," or "to consider." It is significant that Paul used this word in the Greek perfect tense—referring to a completed act with a continuing effect. That is, at some time in the past Paul had considered all of these gains really to be losses—and he still considered them to be losses!

Actually, Paul considered these things to be more than "loss." The Greek word Paul uses (*zēmia*) has the sense of "damage." Think of how the Judaizers would have reacted to such a statement. What they considered to be so significant, Paul not only considered to be a loss but even a damage in comparison to what he had in Jesus Christ. To further strengthen his emphasis, Paul said:

More than that, I count all things to be loss in view of the surpassing value of knowing Christ Jesus my Lord, for whom I have suffered the loss of all things, and count them but rubbish so that I may gain Christ (3:8).

Paul used the same word for "count" in verse 8 as he did in verse 7. However, he used it with another tense to give it a different emphasis. In verse 7 he used the Greek perfect tense to refer to a decision he had made in the past whose effect had continued right up to the present—the time when he was writing. In verse 8, he used the Greek present tense, which emphasizes continuous action in present time. In other words, he was saying, "And I am continually counting all things but loss."

In case the Judaizers thought Paul had changed his mind after his earlier decision, there would be no mistaking how he felt at the present. Paul had no regrets about reaching the decision that his accomplishments in Judaism were entirely worthless in comparison to what he had in Jesus Christ.

He referred to what he presently had in Christ as "the surpassing value of knowing Christ Jesus my Lord" (v. 8). The knowledge of Christ to which Paul referred was a personal knowledge because he had trusted Him as personal Savior. Being in right relationship with Christ by knowing Him personally far surpassed anything Judaism offered. And remember, Paul was one of the most zealous people of his time in the Jewish faith (see Gal. 1:13-14).

Observe Paul's manner of referring to Jesus Christ in Philippians 3:8—"my Lord." No longer was Jesus Christ just a person who lived at a certain time in history as far as Paul was concerned; He was now Paul's Lord.

Having referred to Christ as his Lord, Paul said, "For whom I have suffered the loss of all things" (v. 8). Not only had Paul realized that his accomplishments in Judaism were worthless in comparison to what he had in Christ; it was also a real possibility that he was a social outcast because of his faith in Christ.

Imagine the way his family may have responded when Paul made it known that he believed Jesus Christ was the Messiah that Israel had been waiting for. Paul's stand for Christ probably cost him everything in the way of social standing among his family and relatives, as well as in the Jewish community. But Paul was more than willing to pay this price because of what he had found in Christ.

Further emphasizing the worthlessness of his accomplishments in the Jewish religion, Paul said, "And count them but rubbish so that I may gain Christ" (v. 8). Although the word Paul used for "rubbish" (*skubalon*) can simply mean "refuse," it can also have the meaning of "manure." An example of the word being used as such is cited by Moulton and Milligan in an expression translated "a little bundle and rotten hay, the whole of it decayed—no better than dung [*skubalon*] (*The Vocabulary of the Greek New Testament*, p. 579).

All the former things of life in which Paul had boasted earlier he considered as manure in comparison with the spiritual riches in Christ Jesus. Paul's purpose is indicated at the end of verse 8: "that I may gain Christ." The Greek word translated "gain" here is related to the same word in verse 7. Paul considered the greatest gain to be a right relationship with Jesus Christ, and no one can come into that relationship unless he realizes he is a sinner and has fallen short of God's glory (Romans 3:23). Paul was not referring to working for salvation but was contrasting what the world considers gain with what is really gain. Paul continued to express his relationship with Christ:

And may be found in Him, not having a righteousness of my own derived from *the* Law, but that which is through faith in Christ, the righteousness which *comes* from God on the basis of faith (3:9).

In this verse Paul contrasted the true way of salvation with the false way of salvation being proclaimed by the Judaizers.

Paul commonly referred to believers as those "in Christ," and here he referred to being "in Him." Paul viewed each individual as either in Christ or not in Christ. He was making it clear that his choice was to be "in Him, not having a righteousness of my own."

Paul realized that a righteousness that was one's own was really no righteousness at all. Isaiah 64:6 says, "All our righteous deeds are like a filthy garment." Paul said of his fellow Israelites, "For I testify about them that they have a zeal for God, but not in accordance with knowledge. For not knowing about God's righteousness and seeking to establish their own, they did not subject themselves to the righteousness of God" (Rom. 10:2-3).

So as he wrote to the Philippians, Paul made it clear that a righteousness which is based on the Mosaic Law is not a sufficient righteousness. Of course, the Judaizers were those who based their claim of righteousness on their faithfulness to the Law. The purpose of the Law, however, was never meant to make a person righteous, or to justify him; rather, it was to make him conscious of his sin. Paul also wrote, "Because by the works of the Law no flesh will be justified in His sight; for through the Law *comes* the knowledge of sin" (Rom. 3:20). So when one really seeks righteousness, he does not go to the Law but to Jesus Christ.

Instead of having a righteousness that was based on the

Law, Paul's choice was "that which is through faith in Christ, the righteousness which *comes* from God on the basis of faith" (Phil. 3:9). Here Paul made it clear that righteousness is derived from God—not by keeping a system of laws but by faith in Jesus Christ.

So Paul told the Philippian believers and also the Judaizers that God's righteousness was not to be obtained through works but through faith in Jesus Christ, who paid the penalty for our sin. Paul emphasized this truth over and over again in his writings, especially in the Book of Romans. Paul said, "Being justified as a gift by His grace through redemption which is in Christ Jesus; whom God displayed publicly as a propitiation in His blood through faith. *This* was to demonstrate His righteousness, because in the forbearance of God He passed over the sins previously committed; for the demonstration, *I say*, of His righteousness at the present time, so that He would be just and the justifier of the one who has faith in Jesus" (Rom. 3:24-26).

Chapter 26 –
Advancing with God's
Power

That I may know Him and the power of His resurrection and the fellowship of His sufferings, being conformed to His death (3:10).

PAUL HAD TOLD the Philippians that those things he had had before salvation he later counted as loss because after salvation he had focused his attention on knowing more about Jesus Christ (v. 7-8). Paul did not want to be relying on any righteousness of his own—which really was no righteousness at all—but rather he wanted to rely entirely on the righteousness which he had derived from Jesus Christ by faith (v. 9).

To Paul, salvation was only the beginning, not the end. This is why he said, "That I may know Him." Salvation had delivered him from condemnation, but Paul desperately wanted to know more about Jesus Christ, who died in his place, so that he could have salvation through faith in His shed blood.

Unfortunately, many Christians think that once they have obtained salvation through faith in Christ there is nothing else to pursue. Such believers remain in the infancy stage of the Christian life because they never go on to spiritual maturity.

Writing about Paul's desire to know Christ experientially and intimately, Dr. J. Dwight Pentecost says, "God feeds His children in response to an appetite and a desire, and apart from that desire there will be no feeding. And apart from that feeding, there will be no growth, and apart from that growth, there can never be spiritual maturity. Spiritual giants are not born, they are made" (*The Joy of Living*, p. 138).

Not only did Paul want to know Christ more intimately, he also wanted to know the "power of His resurrection." Notice, it was not just resurrection he wanted to experience; rather, it was the power of Christ's resurrection. The word translated "power" (*dunamis*) refers to power in the sense of "ability." Paul realized the same power that was operable in raising Christ from the dead was the only power that could give him the ability he needed for living the victorious Christian life. This is the same Greek word used in Acts 1:8, where we read that Christ promised the disciples that they would receive power after the coming of the Holy Spirit. The indwelling Holy Spirit gives the believer the ability he needs to be an effective witness for Jesus Christ. Paul wanted to personally experience more of this ability in his life.

Paul also wanted to know the "fellowship of His sufferings" (Phil. 3:10). When the Lord Jesus was on earth, He suffered for the sake of righteousness, and Paul wanted to participate with Him in this suffering. After Paul's conversion on the road to Damascus, the Lord directed Ananias to go to Paul. One of the reasons the Lord gave Ananias for sending him to Paul was this: "For I will show him how much he must suffer for My name's sake" (Acts 9:16). Paul had not drawn back from this suffering; in fact, the Book of Philippians was written several years after his conversion, and even then Paul was still considering it a privilege to fellowship in the sufferings of Christ.

Having stated that he wanted to know Christ, the power of His resurrection and the fellowship of His sufferings, Paul added, "Being conformed to His death" (v. 10). The words "being conformed" are all translated from one Greek word, *summorphizō.* This word emphasizes one's inner essence. Thus, as Paul wrote, he was thinking of the spiritual development of the inner person. The Greek word here is a present participle, which indicates action going on at the same time as the main verb. The main verb is "know," and Paul wanted to know more about Christ, more about the power of His resurrection and more about the fellowship of His sufferings, while being made conformable in his inner man to the death of Christ.

Romans 8:29 reveals what God desires for each believer. Paul said, "For those whom He foreknew, He also predestined to *become* conformed to the image of His Son, so that He would be the firstborn among many brethren." The word translated "conformed" in Romans 8:29 is the same word "conformed" in Philippians 3:10. As Paul learned more about Christ, experienced more of the ability expressed in His resurrection and participated in the fellowship of His sufferings, he knew that these would be used to mold him into the image of Jesus Christ.

In order that I may attain to the resurrection from the dead (3:11).

Some interpreters believe the resurrection Paul referred to was the resurrection of believers. They stress that it is not that Paul doubted whether or not he would be resurrected; rather, his doubt was whether he would be living when Christ returned or would have died by that time. Others see verse 11 in connection with Romans 6, where Paul stressed that believers have died with Christ and have been raised to walk in the newness of life (v.4-5). Either view fits the context of Philippians 3.

Paul's words "in order that" literally mean "if somehow." Paul was not sure of the means, but he had his eyes fixed on the goal, which was that he might "attain to the resurrection from the dead." Paul did not use the common word for "resurrection." Instead, he prefixed the common word with the preposition meaning "out." Thus, it has the idea of the "out resurrection from the dead." As mentioned, some say this is a reference to Romans 6, where the believer is said to have died with Christ and to have been raised with Christ to walk in newness of life. Taking this parallel, one would see Paul's basic desire as wanting to daily experience the resurrection life that Christ has intended for every believer.

Of course, there is a sense that the "out resurrection from the dead" could also refer to the physical resurrection inasmuch as only believers will be resurrected when Christ appears in the air at the end of the Church Age (see 1 Thess. 4:16-17). Since the unsaved are not resurrected at that time, it could be said that the Christians' resurrection is an "out resurrection of the dead." Again, Paul did not doubt that he would be taken home to be with the Lord, but of course, he did not know as he wrote Philippians whether or not he would still be living at the time Christ appeared in the air. When he wrote his last book, 2 Timothy, Paul fully expected to die a martyr's death (4:6). But in case the Philippians thought that Paul had accomplished all in his Christian life that could be accomplished, he added:

Not that I have already obtained *it* or have already become perfect, but I press on so that I may lay hold of that for which also I was laid hold of by Christ Jesus (3:12).

With these words Paul emphasized to the Philippian believers that he had not yet arrived at the final goal; God had not yet accomplished all in his life that He was going to accomplish. In verse 12 Paul seems to be likening his own life to the runners in the Greek games. Paul wanted the Philippians to know that he had not reached the goal at some point in the past; rather, he was still in the process of striving to reach the goal.

Even though Paul had gone on to spiritual maturity by this time in his life, he had not reached a state of absolute perfection such as each believer will have in heaven. The word translated "perfect" can also mean "complete." Paul wanted the believers to know that he was still experiencing difficulties and needed to keep on applying the Word of God to his daily life. The word translated "I press on" (*diōkō*) means "follow" in the sense of "pursue." Like a runner pursuing the goal, Paul wanted to honor Jesus Christ in everything he did so he might be more and more molded into the image of Jesus Christ.

Because Paul had warned the Philippian believers about the legalizers among them who used the Mosaic Law as a checklist of spirituality, it is quite possible that he was contrasting himself with the legalizers in verse 12. Although the legalizers considered themselves to have attained because of their relationship with the Mosaic Law, Paul emphasized that he had not yet come to the place of experiencing all that God had for him.

Paul was following after, or pursuing, "so that I may lay hold of that for which also I was laid hold of by Christ Jesus." The word translated "lay hold of" in both instances is *katalambanō*, meaning "seize, win, attain, make one's own." This Greek word is comprised of a preposition *kata* meaning "down" and *lambanō* meaning "to take." Paul had not yet achieved the complete end in order to say that he had taken it down, or held it down, and made it his own. He believed that Christ still had much more in view for him before his life was brought to a close, at which time he would experience absolute perfection in the presence of Christ.

This is a challenge for each believer to keep his eyes on Christ so that Christ may continue to work in his life as well as through it.

Chapter 27 –
Forgetting – and
Pressing On

Brethren, I do not regard myself as having laid hold of *it* yet; but one thing *I* do: forgetting what *lies* behind and reaching forward to what *lies* ahead (3:13).

PAUL ADDRESSED THE Philippians with an endearing term—"brethren." Although they were not physical brothers, they were spiritual brothers because both they and he had believed in Jesus Christ as personal Savior.

Paul told the Philippians, "I do not regard myself as having laid hold of *it*." The word translated "regard" (*logizomai*) is the same word translated "consider" in Romans 6:11, where Paul told the Roman Christians to "consider yourselves to be dead to sin, but alive to God in Christ Jesus." Both in Romans and in Philippians Paul was presenting facts that are to be counted true because they are true.

Paul told the Philippian believers that he did not consider himself to have "laid hold of." The Greek word involved here is the same one used in verse 12, where it is translated "lay hold of."

Although Paul did not consider that he had yet achieved all that God had in mind for him, he was not lackadaisical in his attitude. Rather, he said, "Forgetting what *lies* behind and reaching to what *lies* ahead, I press on toward the goal for the prize of the upward call of God in Christ Jesus" (v.13-14). Just like a runner in the Greek games of his time, Paul was putting forth every effort as he sought to reach his goal.

Notice that he said, "Forgetting what lies behind" (v. 13). Surely this involves the forgetting of victories as well as defeats—Paul did not want to be controlled by the past; he wanted to press on from the present regardless of the past. Christians sometimes tend to rely on the victories of the past as they seek to live for the Lord in the present. Paul did not want to be guilty of that. On the other hand, some Christians are defeated by the problems of the past and cannot forget them so they can live a life of victory at the present. Paul realized that one could do nothing about the wrongs of the past except confess them to the Lord and then press on from where he presently was.

Imagine some of the problems Paul had as he thought about the past. In his unsaved state he had been guilty of persecuting Christians and even of having some put to death (Acts 22:4), whereas he now recognized that they were brothers in Christ. If anyone would have had a problem with his thought life because of past experiences, it would have been Paul. Yet he chose to deliberately forget what was in the past and to go forward from the present to glorify the Lord.

The word translated "forgetting" is in the present tense, which emphasizes a continual action—he was making it a practice to forget the things in the past. It seems apparent from the context that the idea of "forgetting" especially means he was not relying on the things of the past. Those in Judaism who would covet Paul's natural standing in the world would not be able to imagine how he could disregard all that he had according to the flesh (see Phil. 3:5-6). But Paul did not rely on what he had in the natural realm; his trust was in the Lord, and he was relying on what he had in the spiritual realm.

Not only was Paul forgetting the things which behind, but he was also "reaching forward to what *lies* ahead" (v. 13). Paul seems particularly to have had the runner in view at this time, for the word he used for "reaching" (*epekteinomai*) literally meant "to stretch out" or "to strain." As a runner stretched out to reach the goal first, so Paul was giving his every effort to fulfill the purpose that Jesus Christ chose for him to accomplish. Every runner realizes that the crucial thing is not how far he has come in the race but how much farther he has yet to go. This is why Paul's emphasis was not on the past but on the present and looking ahead to the future.

I press on toward the goal for the prize of the upward call of God in Christ Jesus (3:14).

The intensity with which Paul was moving toward his goal is seen in the word he used for "press." The word is *diōkō*, which also appears in verse 12, where it is translated "press on." But it is much more than a lackadaisical following; it is an intense pursuit. All of Paul's attention was on the goal before him.

But what was Paul's goal? He was intensely pursuing "the prize of the upward call of God in Christ Jesus." The prize, or reward, which Paul sought was the "upward call of God." It was literally an "upward calling" or "calling from above." Interpreters have differed over precisely what this calling involved. Some think it has to do with the calling at the time of salvation concerning the purpose God has for an individual. Others see it as the time of rewards at the end of the Christian life.

Paul may have had both in view because he not only wanted to be faithful in the race, but he also wanted to seek to win the prize. Perhaps Paul had in mind what occurred at the Greek games after a person had successfully run the race. William Hendriksen states: "At the end of the race the successful runner was summoned from the floor of the stadium to the judge's seat to receive the price" (*Philippians*, 9. 174). This was an upward calling because of having been faithful in the race.

Having told about himself and his desire to excel for Jesus Christ, Paul said:

Let us therefore, as many as are perfect, have this attitude; and if in anything you have a different attitude, God will reveal that also to you (3:15).

The word "perfect" was not meant to convey sinless perfection but a desired end, or maturity. The noun is used in verse 15, whereas the verb is used in verse 12, where it is also translated "perfect." Paul was calling on all those who were mature in attitude to think the same way he was thinking. He wanted them to have their minds fixed on the goal of honoring Christ in all they did so that He might be glorified in their lives.

If they had thoughts other than this, Paul realized that he alone could not help them to see the real issues; only God could. But Paul also seemed to have confidence that as long as their desire was to please the Lord, He would reveal to them the areas where their thinking needed correction.

However, let us keep living by that same *standard* to which we have attained (3:16).

Paul was concerned that the Christians in Philippi consistently live according to what they had already attained in the Christian life. Although one is not to rely on past victories for present successes, one should live in a manner consistent with the level of life he has attained for the Lord. Paul was thankful for the Philippian believers and for all they had meant to him. He did not want them to recede in any degree from their spiritual fervor; rather, he wanted them to go on from there to even higher levels. Just as the runner loses precious time if he wavers from the direct path, so Paul wanted the Philippian believers to keep their eyes on the goal and to keep moving forward for Jesus Christ.

Chapter 28 – An Example to Follow

Brethren, join in following my example, and observe those who walk according to the pattern you have in us (3:17).

PAUL ADDRESSED FELLOW believers, as indicated by the word "brethren." He used the plural form of *adelphos*, which was the common word for "brother" in the first century. Although they were not physical brothers, or even fellow Jews, they were brothers in Christ because they and he had trusted Jesus Christ as Savior.

Paul commanded them, "Join in following my example." The word translated "following my example" is *summimētēs* and appears only here in the New Testament. The first three letters of this word have the sense of "with"; whereas the rest of the word is the regular word for "imitator." Paul wanted the Philippians to be imitators with each other, or fellow imitators, of him. Paul could instruct them in such a way because he was an imitator of Jesus Christ.

It is from this word that "mimic" is derived. There is a good sense in which younger believers are to mimic older believers because the older believers should be mimicking Jesus Christ. Peter said, "For you have been called for this purpose, since Christ also suffered for you, leaving an example for you to follow in His steps" (1 Pet. 2:21). When we who know Christ as Savior follow His steps, it is then safe to encourage others to mimic us, even as Paul did. And if we are not following Christ, then we need to deal with the sin in our lives that has taken our eyes off Him.

Paul wanted the Philippians to make it a practice to follow him and to "observe those who walk according to the pattern you have in us" (Phil. 3:17). The word translated "observe" (*skopeō*) means "to look out for," "notice," "keep one's eyes on." Paul wanted the Philippian believers to take special note of those who were walking according to the example he had established. This is the positive element—observing those whose lives are an honor to the Lord Jesus Christ.

The word "pattern" is *tupos*, which had originally referred to a mark left by a blow but later came to have the meaning of "pattern" or "example." Paul's life had served as an outline of the way a Christian life ought to be lived, and many in Philippi were following his example. Paul encouraged believers to take special note of them.

For many walk, of whom I often told you, and now tell you even weeping, *that they* are enemies of the cross of Christ (3:18).

This is the negative aspect—observing those who do not walk in a way that honors the Lord. How interesting that Paul had told the Philippian believers about such people "often." Apparently when discipling these young believers, Paul thought it was important to frequently tell them that there are those who do not live in a way that honors the Lord and are even enemies of the message. Paul saw the instruction as necessary to keep the Philippian believers on target so they would not become spiritually discouraged when they met such people.

Not only did these people dishonor the Lord but they were also "enemies of the cross of Christ." Observe that they were not just enemies of Christ but enemies of the cross of Christ. These individuals to whom Paul was referring may have gone along with the Christian message as long as one talked about the historical Jesus or even the need to follow Him as an example. But when one began talking about the cross, these people soon evidenced that they were enemies of this kind of message.

Probably no other element so focuses attention on the real purpose of Christ's coming to earth as does the cross. Those today who hold a liberal theology do not mind discussing the fact of Christ's coming to earth to demonstrate that He was a great teacher and an example for all to follow. But when one focuses attention on the cross where He shed His blood to pay the penalty of sin, the liberal theologians usually draw the line at this point. They refuse to dwell on what was accomplished at the cross of Christ.

When Paul came to the Corinthians, he had a single goal in mind concerning focusing attention on Christ. Later he told them, "For I determined to know nothing among you except Jesus Christ, and Him crucified" (1 Cor. 2:2). Paul placed his attention on what Christ accomplished when He died on the cross and shed His blood to pay the penalty of sin.

People today find it relatively easy to talk about Christ's coming to be born in a stable and placed in a manger or even to talk of Him as the Savior of the world. But when it comes to talking about what He did on the cross or of recognizing that He died for each individual's sin, this is farther than many people care to go in their thinking.

As Paul wrote to the Philippians, he warned them of those who were enemies of the cross of Christ, saying, "Of whom I often told you, and now tell you even weeping" (Phil. 3:18). What an insight into the heart of the Apostle Paul! He could not write about people being the enemies of the cross of Christ without being broken up emotionally to think of what they were doing to themselves and to Jesus Christ. What they were doing to themselves is evident from the following verse.

Whose end is destruction, whose god is *their* appetite, and *whose* glory is in their shame, who set their minds on earthly things (3:19).

Even though these enemies of the cross of Christ seemed to move about unrestricted at the time Paul wrote, he emphasized that their "end is destruction." Sometimes believers may wonder why enemies of the cross of Christ seem to prosper in this life, but we must not forget that their ultimate end is destruction. Notice that it is not annihilation—they do not cease to exist. It is destruction. Every individual will be somewhere throughout eternity—either in heaven or in hell. Where each person will be depends on his relationship to the Lord Jesus Christ. These about whom Paul was writing were enemies of the cross of Christ and had refused to come into right relationship with Christ by trusting Him as Savior; therefore, their eternal destiny is hell.

Observe their other characteristics: "Whose god is *their* appetite." This may be taken to mean that they lived to gratify their various appetites. Paul said that in the last days people would be "lovers of pleasure rather than lovers of God" (2 Timothy 3:4). This may be what he was referring to in Philippians 3:19—those who live for the pleasures of the moment without any regard for the future.

Some Bible expositors see other possibilities referred to by Paul's use of "appetite." Inasmuch as the Greek word is translated "womb" 12 out of the 22 times it appears in the New Testament, some think Paul was referring to those trusting in natural birth to give them a proper relationship with God. Certainly this was a characteristic of the Jews—they thought because of their physical lineage they had no further need in order to be in right relationship with God. But such thinking was certainly faulty, for the only way any person comes into right relationship with God is by grace through faith in Jesus Christ (see Eph. 2:8-9).

Other expositors think that Paul's emphasis in Philippians 3:19 was concerning those who follow rigid rules and regulations about what they eat. Elsewhere Paul said, "Therefore no one is to act as your judge in regard to food or drink or in respect to a festival or a new moon or a Sabbath day—things which are a *mere* shadow of what is to come; but the substance belongs to Christ" (Col. 2:16-17).

Any of these various views seems to fit the context. These who were enemies of the cross of Christ were obviously trusting in themselves and what they could do rather than trusting in Christ and what He had already done for them.

Paul went on to say about them: "*Whose* glory is in their shame" (Phil. 3:19). As Christians would observe the lives of these individuals, they would see things that were horribly shameful, yet those who were enemies of the cross of Christ were actually glorying in those things. This shows how debased these enemies of the cross had become.

And notice on what these enemies of the cross focused their attention: "Who set their minds on earthly things." They were not concerned about heavenly things, even though they might occasionally talk about them. The basis of all their thinking was that which is earthly rather than that which is heavenly. We see this today in secular humanism of our age. Those who are committed to being able to explain everything apart from a miracle-working God are really enemies of the cross of Christ.

Chapter 29 – The Believer's Perspective

For our citizenship is in heaven, from which also we eagerly wait for a Savior, the Lord Jesus Christ (3:20).

PAUL HAD TOLD the Philippian believers to imitate him and walk according to his example (v. 17). He then went on to explain that some people are actually enemies of the cross of Christ and live only for the things of this earth (vv. 18-19).

To any believer who might wonder why he should follow Paul's example rather than living like the world, Paul explained: "For our citizenship is in heaven" (v. 20). The word translated "citizenship" is *politeuma* and appears only here in the entire New Testament. It is a word which means "commonwealth." The reason why a believer is not to live with only the things of this world in view is that he is actually a citizen of another country—heaven. The believer needs to recognize that his residence on earth is only temporary; therefore, he should not become so attached to it that he treats temporal things as if they were eternal. Paul told the Corinthians: "While we look not at the things which are seen, but at the things which are not seen; for the things which are seen are temporal, but the things which are not seen are eternal" (2 Cor. 4:18).

Hard as it sometimes is for the believer to keep his perspective straight, he must realize that everything he sees is passing; only that which is not seen has eternal significance. Therefore, the qualities one builds into his life are more important than the possessions and pleasures of this world. Having referred to heaven, Paul said, "From which also we eagerly wait for a Savior" (v. 20). The word translated "wait" is *apekdechomai*, meaning "eagerly await." This is also a significant reason why the believer lives differently from the unbeliever. The Christian is expecting Christ to return, which means that a time of reckoning is coming. The non-Christian is unconcerned about a time of accounting because he does not believe that Jesus Christ is returning. Perhaps there is no greater determining factor in the way a person lives than what he thinks about personal accountability.

Those who do not believe that there is any accountability live for the things of this earth because theirs is an eat-drink-and-be-merry philosophy. The Christian, however, expects the Lord to return so he honors Him during this life not only because he knows he will need to give an account but also because he appreciates all that Christ has done for him. The Christian sees that the spiritual qualities of life are what count, not just what one experiences on a human plane.

Paul left no doubt about who the Savior is: "The Lord Jesus Christ" (v. 20). This is the name that is above every name, and Paul said a day is coming when every knee will bow to Him and every tongue shall confess that Jesus Christ is Lord (2:10-11). The lord Jesus Christ is God, and He will ultimately be victorious over all.

Paul then explained what Jesus Christ is someday going to do for believers:

Who will transform the body of our humble state into conformity with the body of His glory, by the exertion of the power that He has even to subject all things to Himself (3:21).

Having mentioned that the Lord Jesus Christ would someday return from heaven, Paul then told what He would do at that time—"who will transform the body of our humble state." Although a different Greek word is used in 1 Corinthians 15:51, Paul there mentioned the change the body would experience at the return of Christ: "We will not all sleep, but we will all be changed." In 1 Corinthians Paul went on to refer to this body of limitation as taking on properties that no longer would experience limitations.

When Paul referred to "our humble state" as he wrote to the Philippians, he was not agreeing with the Greek philosophy of that time. Greek philosophy taught a dualism; that is, matter is evil and the immaterial, or spiritual, is good. The world's philosophy had significantly affected many Christians during the first century. Some thought the body was evil because it is matter and that one should not marry because such a relationship expresses the desire of an evil body. Paul corrected that thinking in 1 Corinthians 7. Apparently it was also thought by some Christians that although the soul and spirit would be taken to be with the Lord, the body would not be since it is evil. Paul wrote 1 Corinthians 15 to counter such erroneous thinking. There he revealed that if there is no such thing as a resurrection body, then Christ has not been raised, and if Christ has not been raised, we are still in our sins (vv.16-17).

The word translated "humble" and used in reference to the body (Phil. 3:21) referred to a "humble station." It is not that the body is evil in itself but that it has been affected by evil. "Therefore, just as through one man sin entered into the world, and death through sin, and so death spread to all men, because all sinned" (Rom. 5:12). Because sin entered the human race, the body of each person experiences degenerative processes which result in death. The only exceptions are those who will be living at the time the Lord Jesus Christ returns in the air, for they will be changed without having to experience death (1 Cor. 15:52). Other persons excepted were Enoch and Elijah, who were taken to heaven without experiencing death.

But all others go the route of physical death because their bodies have been affected by sin.

Paul reminded the Philippians that when Jesus Christ appears, the believer's body would experience change "into conformity with the body of His glory" (Phil. 3:21). What a day it will be when the believer receives a glorified body like the body of the Lord Jesus Christ! It will be a body without limitations and one that will never die. The thought of this led Paul to tell the Corinthians: "But when this perishable will have put on the imperishable, and this mortal will have put on immortality, then will come about the saying that is written, 'Death is swallowed up in victory'" (1 Cor. 15:54).

Because such a concept of a change of one's body is so far beyond human comprehension, the Philippians probably wondered the same as others have wondered: How is this possible? The answer is found in the words that follow: "By the exertion of the power that He has even to subject all things to Himself" (Phil. 3:21). All of this is possible because of the ability of Jesus Christ to bring everything into subjection to Himself. Because He is sovereign over all, Jesus Christ is able to accomplish the changing of a body affected by sin into a glorified body that will never experience decay or limitations.

All of this gives the believer an added impetus to live with eternity's values in view rather than with only the pleasures of this world in view.

Chapter 30 – Standing Fast Yet Working Together

Therefore, my beloved brethren whom I long *to see*, my joy and crown, in this way stand firm in the Lord, my beloved (4:1).

HAVING EMPHASIZED TO the believers in Philippi that their citizenship was a heavenly one and that Christ would eventually subdue all things to Himself (3:20-21), Paul had something especially important he wanted to state in Chapter 4.

He began by reminding the believers in Philippi that they were "beloved brethren whom I long to see" (4:1). The word translated "beloved" (*agapētos*) was an especially endearing term which revealed Paul's deep affection for the believers in Philippi. Acts 16 tells of the response Paul had when he proclaimed the gospel in Philippi, and it also tells of the beating and imprisonment Paul had suffered there. But regardless of the trials Paul experienced, those who came to Christ through his ministry remained "beloved" to him.

He also referred to them as "whom I long to see" (Phil. 4:1), and here he used a word (*epipothētos*) which emphasized a strong desire. This word reveals how much Paul yearned for Christian fellowship, especially with those he had discipled for Christ.

Paul also referred to the believers in Philippi as "my joy and crown" (4:1). These people were an obvious delight to Paul's heart, and he considered them to be a choice fruit of his ministry. The word Paul used for "crown" (*stephanos*) referred to a victor's crown. He had been in spiritual warfare for these believers and considered them to be the results of victory.

It is significant to notice also that the words "my joy and crown" imply that Paul had a people-centered ministry. No doubt Paul used the best methods available to him in evangelizing and following up his converts, but he never lost sight of the fact that everything he did was for people. This is also emphasized in his first letter to the Thessalonians, for he said, "For who is our hope or joy or crown of exultation? Is it not even you, in the presence of our Lord Jesus at His coming? For you are our glory and joy" (1 Thess. 2:19-20).

Having expressed to the Philippian believers that he considered them his joy and crown, Paul urged: "Stand firm in the Lord, my beloved" (Phil. 4:1). Paul did not want the Philippians to be shaken in their faith by problems they were encountering in their group or by the persecution by unbelievers. Since there had been such a reaction to Paul and Silas as they preached the gospel in Philippi (Acts 16), it is only reasonable to assume that the Philippian believers experienced persecution for their faith after Paul and Silas left. Thus, Paul encouraged them to "stand firm in the Lord" (Phil. 4:1). Even though Paul had used his knowledge to communicate information to the Philippians, Paul urged them to stand firm "in the Lord," not in the wisdom of men. Having said this, Paul then came to an intensely personal part of his letter to the Philippians:

I urge Euodia and I urge Syntyche to live in harmony in the Lord (4:2).

The fact that these two names are in the feminine gender

reveals that Paul was referring to two women. This is the only time that either of these women is mentioned in the entire New Testament. Possibly they were among the early converts when Paul first visited Philippi, but their names are not specifically mentioned in Acts 16.

Paul was particularly concerned that these two women "live in harmony" (Phil. 4:2). Literally translated, Paul said, "To think the same thing." Paul used the same Greek word here as he did in 2:2 where he told the Philippians to be "of the same mind."

Notice the sphere about which Paul was concerned that Euodia and Syntyche be of the same mind—"in the Lord" (4:2). Although Paul did not give any specifics about the differences of these women, it is implied that they did not have the same goals in mind concerning serving the Lord, or perhaps they had different plans in mind as to how to reach those goals, so they were unable to work together in harmony. Although believers will never think exactly alike, they should agree in their local ministry and should be willing to give ground on ways to reach these goals. Any time a person becomes part of a group, it is necessary for him or her to give up some personal opinions if there is going to be harmony in the group.

Paul believed the need for these women to come to common terms was so urgent that he even sought outside help:

Indeed, true companion, I ask you also to help these women who have shared my struggle in *the cause of* the gospel, together with Clement also and the rest of my fellow workers, whose names are in the book of life (4:3).

As Paul sought for a third party to help resolve the differences between Euodia and Syntyche, he referred to one as a "true companion." Some commentators think that Paul was referring to a specific person by the name of Suzuge, which means yokefellow. Others think that it would have been obvious to the person to whom Paul was referring and that he was simply using a descriptive word in referring to him rather than his name. In either case, Paul appealed to him to help heal the division between the two women.

That these women were not just new Christians is indicated by what Paul said about them: "These women who have shared my struggle in *the cause of* the gospel." They had been co-workers with the veteran apostle, yet something or someone had divided them so that they were no longer able to work together. No doubt Paul recognized that it was a hindrance to the work in Philippi for these older Christians to be at odds with each other. Their differences needed to be healed not only for their own sakes but also for the sake of the Christian witness in Philippi.

These women had worked not only with Paul but also with Clement, who is mentioned only here in the New Testament. And, Paul added, "And the rest of my fellow workers, whose names are in the book of life." Paul was not questioning the salvation of these two women who had labored with others whose names were in the Book of Life, but he was obviously concerned about who was controlling their lives. To the Corinthians, Paul had written that divisions result from carnality. He said, "For you are still fleshly. For since there is jealousy and strife among you, are you not fleshly, and are you not walking like mere men?" (1 Cor. 3:3).

Since Paul believed that carnality results in divisions, he was surely thinking as he wrote to the Philippians that either Euodia or Syntyche, or even both of them, had become carnal—living to please themselves rather than seeking to please Jesus Christ.

What a sobering reminder this is that we whose names are in the Book of Life and who have worked closely together can harm our personal relationships and hinder the work of Christ whenever we live for self rather than for Christ.

Chapter 31 – The Answer to Worry

Rejoice in the Lord always; again I will say, rejoice! (4:4).

WHAT A COMMAND Paul gave to the Philippians and to all believers! It would have been one thing if he had emphasized occasional rejoicing, but Paul used a tense for the word "rejoice" which emphasized continual rejoicing. And, as if that were not enough, he said "always" or "at all times."

If anyone else had written such a statement, believers might have thought that the author did not realize the significance of what he was saying. But the Apostle Paul had been through severe trials, had been to the point of death and was in prison even as he wrote these words. It is likely that he dragged a chain across the desk with his hand as he wrote: "Rejoice in the Lord always; again I will say, rejoice!" This man who had been through so much for the Lord not only commanded believers to continually rejoice at all times but even repeated his command: "Again I will say, rejoice!"

Throughout the next few verses Paul made statements that are possible to apply in a person's life only if he has strong confidence in God. In order to be able to rejoice in every situation, a believer must be convinced that God knows what He is doing and that He makes no mistakes. Paul had such confidence in God, and no one could rob him of it.

Let your gentle *spirit* be known to all men. The Lord is near (4:5).

Paul wanted believers to live in such a way that others would know their gentleness. The Greek word that is translated "gentle" has many shades of meaning. Hendrickson, in his commentary on Philippians, prefers the translation of "big-heartedness" and says one may substitute any of the following: "forbearance, yieldedness, geniality, kindliness, gentleness, sweet reasonableness, considerateness, charitableness, mildness, magnanimity, generosity" (p. 193).

Perhaps one might say that this word incorporates all the fruit of the Spirit—"love, joy, peace, patience, kindness, goodness, faithfulness, gentleness, self-control" (Gal. 5:22-23).

Notice that Paul did not consider it sufficient for a person to have moderation; Paul wanted that moderation to "be known to all men" (Phil. 4:5). In essence, Paul was urging the Philippian believers to be good witnesses. He wanted them to have the right kind of life, and then he wanted that life to be made evident to others in everyday living.

Paul underscored the urgency of this matter by saying, "The Lord is near" (v. 5). The testimony of the Scriptures is that the Lord can come at any time, and this is why the believer should be alert and capitalizing on spiritual opportunities. No one knows how much time he has left, and though he plans for the future, he should live as if each day might be the last. When one remembers that he might soon stand before the Lord, this can change the way he lives. After referring to meeting the Lord face to face, the Apostle John said, "And everyone who has this hope *fixed* on Him purifies himself, just as He is pure" (1 John 3:3).

Be anxious for nothing, but in everything by prayer and supplication with thanksgiving let your requests be made known to God (4:6).

Perhaps no verse has been more convicting to Christians than this one. Almost every believer is sensitive to the fact that he or she worries about what might happen in the future.

Some then wonder if there is a difference between concern and worry. There seems to be such a difference because, in his letter to the Galatians, Paul told believers to be concerned about the things of others: "Bear one another's burdens, and thereby fulfill the law of Christ" (Gal. 6:2). Yet, this is different from being obsessed with what might happen in the future.

The word translated "be anxious for" (*merimnaō*) means "to be troubled with cares." From the context it is apparent that Paul was trying to help believers so they would not always be worrying about the future.

Paul included everything when he said, "In everything by prayer and supplication with thanksgiving let your requests be made known to God" (Phil. 4:6). Again it should be said that the only way a person can have such a relaxed attitude in the midst of circumstances he does not understand is to realize that God is sovereign and that His will is being accomplished. No doubt this is why Paul so closely linked the matter of rejoicing in everything and the matter of not being distressed over anything with the aspect of praying to God about everything.

In this verse are three words which relate to prayer. The first one, which is translated "prayer" is *proseuchē*, and though it is a common word for prayer, it always means prayer addressed to God. The word translated "supplication" (*deēsis*) emphasizes a sense of need. The word is used of requests from one person of another as well as of people requesting things from God. The third word translated "requests (*aitēma*) and refers to something asked, or a petition. Three words seem to move from the general to the particular and emphasize the importance of believers being specific in their prayers.

Notice, however, that all praying or asking is to be done "with thanksgiving." The believer is to thank God not only for the answers in the past but also for the answers that will come in the future. Again one sees Paul's emphasis on the need to have confidence in the sovereignty of God so that the individual Christian does not panic as he brings his needs before God. The result of such an attitude and prayer is seen in the following verse:

And the peace of God, which surpasses all comprehension, will guard your hearts and your minds in Christ Jesus (4:7).

In the midst of turmoil and extreme circumstances, every believer can have God's peace in his life. This verse reveals that personal peace is not dependent on circumstances; rather, it is dependent on one's personal relationship with the Lord. When one realizes that God is in control and does not make mistakes, this gives him a peace that he is not able to obtain in any other way.

Just as Roman soldiers protected those within from those without, so the peace of God protects the believer from those things which would render him ineffective for the Lord.

Though difficult to apply, these verses show that the answer to worry is a prayer life that is based on confidence in the sovereignty of God. Nor is the person able to explain his peace to someone else. Paul said, this peace "surpasses all comprehension"; that is, it goes beyond what anyone is able to understand. A life that evidences the peace of God is an argument that unbelievers cannot explain away.

This peace goes beyond all comprehension, and notice what it does. Paul said this peace, "will guard your hearts and your minds in Christ Jesus." For the words "will guard" Paul used a Greek word that was common in the days of the Roman Empire: *phroureō*. This word referred to protecting by guarding. The Philippians would have been familiar with the Roman soldiers who stood guard at various important places in the Empire. Those within a guarded building need have no worry concerning what was on the outside as long as the Roman soldiers were there. So, too, the heart that has the peace of God does not need to worry about what might happen.

Chapter 32 – The Believer's Thought Life

Finally, brethren, whatever is true, whatever is honorable, whatever is right, whatever is pure, whatever is lovely, whatever is of good repute, if there is any excellence and if anything worthy of praise, dwell on these things (4:8).

PAUL HERE USED the word *loipon* with the article *to*, which is translated "finally," as he also did in 3:1. The word "finally" is too narrow in meaning for *loipon* as it can also mean simply "the remaining" or "the rest" as well as "besides" or "moreover." In the context of 4:8 it seems best to take it to mean "besides" or "moreover."

Paul had just told the Philippian believers not to worry but to take everything to God in prayer (v. 6). Paul assured them that if they did this, the peace of God would guard their hearts and minds (v. 7). In addition to these instructions, Paul then added the exhortation contained in verse 8.

The purpose of Paul's statements in verse 8 was to help the believers know what they should allow their minds to dwell on. That his instructions were specifically addressed to believers is evident from his use of the word "brethren" (*adelphoi*). Unbelievers cannot be expected to heed Paul's injunctions in verse 8 because their minds have been blinded by Satan, "the god of this world" (2 Cor. 4:4). Not until a person trusts Christ as Savior and is empowered by the indwelling Holy Spirit is he able to have victory in his thought life.

The believer is not to open his mind to just any thought but is to bring "every thought captive to the obedience of Christ" (2 Cor. 10:5). What should a believer think about? The answer is Philippians 4:8.

Paul said, "Whatever is true" (Phil. 4:8). This is the first in a series of six quality items for thought. The word translated "true" is *alēthē*, which has the sense of that which is factually true in contrast to that which is false. No distinction should be drawn between spiritual truth and secular truth—all truth is God's truth. The believer should think on those things which are true, not on those which are false.

Paul also said, "Whatever is honorable" (v. 8). The word "honorable" is too limited in meaning today to reveal the full sense of what Paul intended by his use of the word *semnos*. The Greek word had the meaning of that which is worthy of respect. It is used in the New Testament only here and in 1 Timothy 3:8, 11 and Titus 2:2. Trench suggests that the word combines the elements of gravity and dignity which invites reverence (*Synonyms of the New Testament*, p. 348).

The third quality Paul stipulated for the believer to think on was "whatever is right" (Phil. 4:8). Paul's word for "right" was *dikaios*. Which also means "righteous." It refers to that which corresponds to the divine standard. That which is right is what the believer is to think about.

To this Paul added: "Whatever is pure" (v. 8). Although it is common to think of the 21th century as the most decadent time in history, the Roman world of Paul's day was also a sex-saturated society. Many of the first-century believers were saved out of idol worship which had prostitutes for priestesses, and it was necessary for Paul and other Scripture writers to emphasize the need for purity. When the mind is permitted to drift, it often settles on that which is impure, but the believer is to see to it that the mind remains on that which is pure. The Greek word Paul used was *hagnos*, which also means "holy."

"Whatever is lovely" (v. 8) was another qualification. Paul's word for "lovely" was *prosphilē*, which also means "pleasing" and "agreeable." Believers are to think on that which produces and keeps harmony rather than on that which causes strife.

Paul's sixth qualification was "whatever is of good repute" (v. 8). Moulton and Milligan suggest that in this context the word *euphēmos* (good report) "signifies the delicacy which guards the lips, that nothing may be expressed in public worship that could disturb devotion or give rise to scandal" (*The Vocabulary of the Greek New Testament*, p. 267).

Having mentioned six qualifications for that which believers are to think about, Paul summarized by saying, "If there is any excellence and if anything worthy of praise, dwell on these things" (v. 8). The word "if" does not suggest doubt in Paul's mind, for in the sentence construction he used, it has the meaning of "since" or "because." It is like telling a Christian, "If you are a believer, you should study the Bible." Because there are virtue (moral excellence) and praise (things worthy of praise) in the qualities listed by Paul, the believer is commanded to "dwell on these things" (v. 8).

Paul's word for "dwell" was *logizomai*, which means "reckon," "calculate" or "consider." The believer is to consider or let his mind dwell on that which meets these qualifications. This is scriptural positive thinking. Paul used the word in the Greek present tense, indicating that the believer is to continuously consider these things.

The things you have learned and received and heard and seen in me, practice these things, and the God of peace will be with you (4:9).

Whereas in verse 8 Paul instructed believers what to think about, in verse 9 he told them what to do. It is significant that Paul thought it important to treat the area of the mind before specifying actions. More Christians are defeated in the battle for the mind than in the area of actions. However, proper actions are the result of proper thinking.

In verse 9 Paul seems to divide learning into two areas: (1) learning and receiving, and (2) hearing and seeing. The first couplet focused attention on the Philippians, the last on Paul.

The Philippian believers had "learned" (*manthanō*) as Paul gave them information during his brief stay with them (see Acts 16:12-40). But it was much more than just information to them—they also received it. Paul's word for "received" was *paralambanō*, which was the common word for receiving something. In the context it implies that they responded to the information by taking it to themselves.

In addition, the Philippians had heard and seen things in Paul's life (v. 8). He had been an example to them as he had suffered imprisonment and had taught them the truth of God. Taking into consideration everything the Philippians had learned by all means, Paul commanded, "Practice these things" (v. 9).

The word Paul used for "practice" was *prassō*. In addition to the word's inherent meaning of constantly doing, Paul put it in the Greek present tense to emphasize continuous action. Thus, Paul made a double emphasis on the Philippians' need to constantly demonstrate in their actions all they had learned.

To Paul it was not enough that the Philippians had gained more knowledge—he wanted to see a change of behavior that resulted from that knowledge. Paul wanted them to go on to maturity. J. Dwight Pentecost makes this discerning remark: "Maturity in the Christian life is not measured by what a man knows but by what he does" (*The Joy of Living*, p. 212).

Note what happens when a believer practices what he or she knows: "The God of peace will be with you" (v. 9). In verse 7 Paul referred to the "peace of God," but now he referred to the "God of peace." It is impossible to have one without the other. The blessing of God is on the believer who hungrily seeks to learn more about God and then translates that knowledge into daily living.

Chapter 33 – Secret of Paul's Contentment

But I rejoiced in the Lord greatly, that now at last you have revived your concern for me; indeed, you were concerned *before*, but you lacked opportunity (4:10).

PAUL HERE EXPRESSES his gratitude for the gift which the Philippian believers had sent to him by the hand of Epaphroditus. The Philippians had sent Epaphroditus to Rome to be of help to Paul during his imprisonment and to take a financial gift to him.

When Epaphroditus brought the Philippians' gift, Paul "rejoiced" (4:10). The word translated "rejoiced" here (*chairō*) is used by Paul nine times in his letter to the Philippians. A related word (*chara*) is used five times. So it is easy to see that one of the main themes of the Book of Philippians is "joy" or "rejoicing," in spite of the fact that Paul was writing from a prison which was probably a damp dungeon where he was under constant surveillance.

Paul not only rejoiced, but he also rejoiced greatly because of his assistance the Philippians had sent. It would have been sufficient for the Philippians to know Paul rejoiced because of their gift; surely they were impressed to know he *greatly* rejoiced because of their gift.

But notice the sphere of Paul's rejoicing—he rejoiced "in the Lord" (*en kurios*). Paul constantly emphasized positional truth—what believers are in Christ, or are in the Lord. Here he acknowledged that this financial gift from the Philippians was another blessing from God, so he rejoiced in the Lord.

Paul was grateful that the Philippians' care, or concern, had "revived" (4:10). The word Paul used for "revived" was *anathallō*, which meant "to grow again." The word appears only here in the New Testament. Paul viewed the concern of the Philippians as always existing but now breaking into blossom like a flower as they had opportunity to express their love for him.

The probable reason the Philippians were not able to express their love in visible ways more often was that they were living under poverty conditions themselves. They were among the churches in Macedonia of whom Paul said in 2 Corinthians 8:2, 4: "That in a great ordeal of affliction their abundance of joy and their deep poverty overflowed in the wealth of their liberality…begging us with much urging for the favor of participation in the support of the saints."

In 2 Corinthians 8, Paul mentioned that the churches of Macedonia had given gifts to him so he could pass them on to those in need. In Philippians 4 the gift appears to have been given specifically to Paul for his needs. Although Paul knew the Philippians would have liked to help him before, he realized they "lacked opportunity" (v. 10), which probably means he knew they had no money to give.

Paul was so thrilled with the gift from the Philippians that one might think he was more concerned about material means than he should have been. But he left no doubt about his attitude toward material gain when he said:

Not that I speak from want, for I have learned to be content in whatever circumstances I am (4:11).

Paul was obviously in need as he was in prison in Rome, but he wanted to make sure the Philippians understood that the true cause of his rejoicing was not his desire for more money. He said he had "learned" (*manthanō*) to be content in all conditions. It was something he had learned because he was likely from a wealthy Jewish family in which he had an affluent first-century life-style. This is indicated by Philippians 4:12, where he said, "I know how to live in prosperity." It is also indicated by the fact that he was trained at the feet of Gamaliel (Acts 22:3), a privilege which probably cost significantly and thus was afforded only by the wealthy.

But Paul had given up such standing and affluence when he had chosen to follow Jesus Christ (Phil. 3:8), and he had learned by experience to be content with little even when he had been content with much.

"In whatever circumstances" (4:11) has reference to "things." In whatever circumstances Paul found himself, he was able to adjust to them—he had learned to be content. The word translated "content" is *autarkēs* which, though having a meaning of "self-sufficient," also had the meaning of "content." The context makes it clear that Paul did not consider his ability to adjust to adverse circumstances to be of his own strength.

To emphasize the variety of conditions he had experienced, Paul said:

I know how to get along with humble means, and I also know how to live in prosperity; in any and every circumstance I have learned the secret of being filled and going hungry, both of having abundance and suffering need (4:12).

Paul knew what it was to be "humble." Paul used the same word in referring to Christ, who gave up the glory He had with the Father and "humbled himself" (Phil. 2:8). If the Master humbled Himself, surely it is to be expected that the servants would also face humbling circumstances. Paul told about some of those circumstances in 2 Corinthians 11:23-33.

But Paul also knew what it was like to "live in prosperity" (Phil. 4:12); that is, to have more than enough. He probably referred here to his family life before he became a Christian, but he probably also referred to times when he had learned to live on less and more was provided by the Lord than his immediate need.

In verse 11 Paul said he had learned to be content. In verse 12 he said, "In any and every circumstance I have learned." The word "learned" is *mueō*, which meant "to initiate," but which also had the sense of "to learn the secret." Although there were secrets in the mystery religions of Paul's day, there were also secrets a person could learn in Christianity—and one of those was how to be content regardless of one's circumstances.

Paul said he had learned the secret "of being filled and going hungry, both of having abundance and suffering need" (4:12). Paul singled out different aspects of life as he continued to emphasize why his rejoicing greatly over the Philippians' gift did not depend on his circumstances alone.

After receiving Paul's letter, the Philippians might wonder—and many Christians today might wonder—How was all of this possible, Paul? How does one learn the secret of being content in every kind of circumstance? Paul answered the question in the following verse:

I can do all things through Him who strengthens me (4:13).

This is perhaps one of the most quoted verses from the Book of Philippians. But did Paul intend it to be used without limitations? Paul was not referring to doing something in the sense of learning a particular profession. Some today might say, "If you want to become an accomplished musician or medical doctor, you can, because you can do all things through Christ."

It is true that Christ gives motivation and discipline so a person might accomplish unusual achievements, but this was not what Paul was referring to in this context. He had learned that he could adjust to all things through Christ. It was not Paul's efforts that gave him the ability to adjust—it was Christ who strengthened him.

The word translated "strengthens" is *endunamoō* which, in addition to "strengthen," also meant "able" or "enable." Christ is the One who had enabled Paul to be content in all kinds of circumstances. Contentment is not determined by what a person has but by what his or her relationship is to Jesus Christ.

Chapter 34 – They "Communicated" With Paul

Nevertheless, you have done well to share *with me* in my affliction (4:14).

PAUL HAD THANKED the Philippians for their gift (v. 10) and then had explained that with God's enabling he had learned to adjust to circumstances of poverty and plenty (vv. 11-13). In explaining how he had adjusted through God's help and that he did not consider himself in need, Paul was concerned that the Philippians not consider him ungrateful. So he said, "Nevertheless, you have done well" (v. 14).

Even though he was not in desperate need, he commended the Philippians for sending him a gift. The adverb translated "well" is *kalōs*, meaning "good," but it can also have the sense of "excellently" or "nobly." They had done far more than what might be expected, and Paul was highly pleased by their demonstration of love.

Paul said, "You have done well to share *with me* in my affliction" (v. 14). The Greek word translated "share" is *sugkoinōneō* meaning "to participate in with someone." They were so concerned about Paul that they considered his suffering to be their suffering. They knew by experience what Paul stated in 1 Corinthians 12:26: "If one member suffers, all the members suffer with it."

Having commended the Philippians for their act of love, Paul reminded them:

You yourselves also know, Philippians, that at the first preaching of the gospel, after I left Macedonia, no church shared with me in the matter of giving and receiving but you alone (4:15).

Paul reminded his readers that only the church in Philippi had helped him financially after he had been in Macedonia (present-day northern Greece) preaching the gospel.

On his second missionary journey, the Apostle Paul, through a vision, received a call to come over to Macedonia to help those there. He did so, and one of the first cities he and his companions visited was Philippi. After making converts and having a prison experience (Acts 16:12-31), Paul and his fellow workers visited other locations in Macedonia. They passed through Amphipolis and Apollonia and then came to Thessalonica, where unbelieving Jews drove them from the city (17:1-9). Paul and his companions then went to Berea, but the unbelieving Jews came from Thessalonica and caused animosity among the people, so the Christians sent Paul out of Macedonia (vv. 10-15).

As Paul wrote back to the Philippian believers, he pointed out that this young church had helped him financially even during the brief time he was in Macedonia. Paul referred to "the first preaching of the gospel" (Phil. 4:15). From the context, Paul here referred to the gospel's beginning in Macedonia. From the time when the gospel first came there and they were converted to Christ, the Philippians had helped Paul with financial gifts.

"The first preaching of the gospel" in 4:15 is a reminder of what Paul wrote in 1:5, where he thanked God for the Philippians' "participation in the gospel from the first day until now." Their participation and concern had been demonstrated by specific acts of giving to help meet Paul's needs.

Paul explained to the Philippians that when he was departing from Macedonia (from Thessalonica to Berea to the sea), no church "shared with me in the matter of giving and receiving but you alone" (4:15). The words "giving and receiving" (*doseōs kai lēmpseōs*) were a bookkeeping expression relating to credit and debit. It was as if Paul was saying, "No other church opened an account with me except you."

Paul then mentioned specifically some of the acts of giving he referred to:

For even in Thessalonica you sent a gift more than once for my needs (4:16).

After Paul had left Philippi after being released from prison, he had gone out to Thessalonica, where he met fierce opposition from the unbelieving Jews. But what a joy it must have been for him in the midst of this opposition to receive a gift from those he had just led to the Lord.

The Philippians had received spiritual blessings through Paul, and they responded by sharing with him their material possessions. They were practicing what Paul had instructed the Galatians: "The one who is taught the word is to share all good things with the one who teaches *him*" (Gal. 6:6).

In Philippians 4:16 Paul said the believers had sent "more than once" (*hapax kai dis*), or literally, "once and twice." In the light of the fact that Paul was in Thessalonica less than a month (Acts 17:2), it is significant that the Philippians sent two gifts in such a short time.

Although Paul had stressed that he did not "speak from want" (Phil. 4:11), he said that the Philippians' gifts were sent to his "necessity," or need. He gratefully used the gifts presented to him, but he did not spend his time bemoaning his situation and concentrating on his needs. His satisfaction was derived not from circumstances but from his relationship with Jesus Christ. What an example he was to all believers!

Chapter 35 –
Worshipful Giving

Not that I seek the gift itself, but I seek for the profit which increases to your account (4:17).

PAUL WAS PLEASED that the Christians in Philippi had expressed their concern for him in a tangible way (v. 10). However, he assured them that his gratitude was not simply because of his need, for he had, by the grace of God, learned to adjust to circumstances of poverty as well as to circumstances of plenty (vv.11-13). As Paul touched on both aspects—his gratitude for their gift and his contentment even with little—he wanted to emphasize that the Philippians had done something highly commendable in sharing their financial means with him (v. 14).

Even when he was in Thessalonica, which was only a short time after he had been in Philippi, the Philippians had sent financial gifts to him at least twice (v. 16), and after he had left the area altogether, they had continued to send gifts to him (v. 15).

Having expressed his gratitude for their most recent gift, Paul explained why he was so pleased with their gift: "Not that I seek the gift itself" (v. 17). Again, he made sure they understood that he was not moping around in a discouraged state because of his material needs. The word translated "seek" (*epizēteō*) meant "to inquire for." None of Paul's words or actions were to be interpreted by the Philippians as indicating that he was seeking financial gifts from them.

Paul went on to say why he rejoiced so much over their gift: "But I seek for the profit which increases to your account" (v. 17). Although Paul was grateful for the help the gift was to him, he was more thankful because the gift would be credited to their account. The word translated "account" (*logos*) is the same word that occurs in verse 15 in the phrase "in the matter of giving and receiving," for it was a first-century business expression. In verse 17 Paul referred to credit placed on the account of the Philippians because of their gift. How strange! A gift intended to benefit the receiver became an even greater benefit to the giver! How can this be? The answer is in verse 18.

But I have received everything in full and have an abundance; I am amply supplied, having received from Epaphroditus what you have sent, a fragrant aroma, an acceptable sacrifice, well-pleasing to God (4:18).

Even though Paul did not seek a gift because the Lord had enabled him to adjust to all kinds of circumstances, now that he had received a gift, he considered himself as having all and as abounding. The reason for his state of fullness was that Epaphroditus had brought gifts to him from the Philippians.

Paul had mentioned Epaphroditus previously in his letter to the Philippians (2:25-30). The Philippians had sent Epaphroditus to Paul to minister to his needs (v. 25). But Epaphroditus became sick and nearly died while with Paul (vv. 26-27). Paul was sending Epaphroditus back to Philippi and urged the believers there to receive him with gladness and to hold him in high regard (v. 29).

In Paul's reference to what he had received from Epaphroditus, notice what he said concerning the gifts: "A fragrant aroma" (4:18). Paul was most likely referring to the burnt, meal (or grain) and peace offerings mentioned in

Leviticus 1-3. There offerings were voluntary acts of worship and considered a sweet savor to the Lord. Paul viewed the gifts sent to him by the Philippians to be voluntary acts of worship of the Lord and thus, they were "a fragrant aroma, an acceptable sacrifice, well-pleasing to God" (v. 18). This is why Paul was so pleased with the gifts—He knew God was pleased with them and that God would credit these gifts to the account of the Philippians.

This passage provides a scriptural basis for saying that giving to meet the needs of those in the Lord's work is an act of worship of God. Such gifts are a "fragrant aroma, an acceptable sacrifice, well-pleasing to God" (v. 18).

In that the Philippians had been so concerned in helping to meet Paul's needs, he assured them of what God would do in their behalf.

And my God will supply all your needs according to His riches in glory in Christ Jesus (4:19).

This familiar verse has been both used and misused by many Christians. Some use it to obligate God to meet their desires in whatever area they care to specify. Yet, notice in the context that it emphasizes one particular reason for God's meeting the needs of the Philippians. They had given of their means to support one in the Lord's work, and because of that Paul was confident that God would meet their needs. Surely it is legitimate to extend the principle not only beyond giving to those in the Lord's work but also to the expenses involved in the Lord's work itself. However, it must be kept in mind that Paul's confidence about God's meeting the needs of others was directly related to their being good stewards of the money God had entrusted to them. There is no license here for being irresponsible in financial affairs and yet thinking that God is obligated to meet a person's needs just because he is a Christian.

God does not simply give out of His riches, He gives "according to" them. There is no limit to God's riches. He does not just give believers enough to meet individual situations, but He has "blessed us with every spiritual blessing in the heavenly *places* in Christ" (Eph. 1:3). As the believer honors God in his daily walk—by being a good steward of all that God has committed to him—God will meet his "needs according to His riches in glory in Christ Jesus" (Phil. 4:19).

Chapter 36 – Paul's Concluding Words to the Philippians

Now to our God and Father be the glory forever and ever. Amen (4:20).

PAUL HAD EXPRESED his gratitude to the Christians at Philippi for their most recent gift. Although they were living on a poverty level, they had used the little they had to help him because he had spiritually helped them. Paul was pleased with their gift, not only because of the help it was to him but especially because the giving would be credited to their account (4:17).

Since the Philippians had been responsive to the Lord and had given out of their poverty, Paul assured them that God would meet their needs (v. 19). Apparently these words of Paul to the Philippians about God's giving nature caused emotion to well within him, and he broke into the doxology of verse 20: "Now to our God and Father be the glory forever and ever. Amen." Hendricksen well observes concerning Paul's expression in this verse: "For Paul, doctrine is never a dry matter. Whenever it occupies his mind, it also fills his heart with praise" (*Philippians*, p. 210).

In the construction of the Greek language of verse 20, the words "God" and "Father" follow one article (the). Thus, according to the rules of Greek Grammar, both of these words refer to the same person.

And concerning this divine person, Paul said that to Him should be "glory forever and ever" (v. 20). The Greek word for "glory" is *doxa*, from which the word "doxology" is derived. Paul wanted praise and honor to be given the Heavenly Father because of His care for His own children, even as Paul had assured the Philippians that God would take care of their needs (4:19).

Paul was so elated concerning the goodness of God that he wanted glory to be given to Him not only for time but also for eternity—"forever and ever."

Having given this benediction because of the goodness of God, Paul drew to a close his letter to the Philippians. The remaining verses contain exchanges of greetings and a complimentary close to the letter.

Greet every saint in Christ Jesus. The brethren who are with me greet you (4:21).

Paul wanted the readers of his letter to pass on greetings to every believer they met. The word "saint" has connotations today that were not true of the word Paul used. He used the word *hagios*, which referred to a person set apart to God. The pagan world used the word in Paul's time to refer to a person set apart to the gods, but Paul was using it in referring to one set apart to the true God.

The words that are commonly translated "sanctify" and "holy" come from Greek words related to this one for "saint." The person who recognizes that Christ has died to pay the penalty for his sin and who trusts Christ as his personal Savior qualifies as a saint in the New Testament sense of the term.

Although the geographical location of each saint to whom Paul referred was in Philippi, the spiritual location of each believer was "in Christ Jesus" (v. 21). This terminology is used only of believers living during the Church Age; that is, from the Day of Pentecost, as recorded in Acts 2, forward. No

Old Testament saint was ever referred to as being "in Christ." During this present Church Age all the blessings of God are made available to the believer "in Christ" (Eph. 1:3).

Paul also told the Philippian believers, "The brethren who are with me greet you" (Phil. 4:21). Some interpreters have thought there were no other believers with Paul because of what he said in 2:19-21 concerning sending Timothy to them because none other was available. However, Paul did not say no other believers were available; rather, he said no one was available and willing to go who was qualified as Timothy was.

In conveying greetings, Paul went on to say:

All the saints greet you, especially those of Caesar's household (4:22).

Having referred to "the brethren who are with me" (v. 21), Paul enlarged the scope to include "all the saints" (v. 22). Apparently any believer who even came into contact with Paul wanted to be remembered to the Christians in Philippi. Nothing in the text indicates why there was such a strong interest in those in Philippi.

But of "all the saints," Paul singled out "especially those of Caesar's household" (v. 22). The reference to "household," according to A.T. Robertson, included "not members of the imperial family, but some connected with the imperial establishment. The term can apply to slaves and freedmen and even to the highest functionaries" (*Word Pictures in the New Testament*, Vol. IV, p. 463).

This reference to Caesar's household is one of the indications that Paul's letter to the Philippians was written from Rome, the imperial headquarters. If Paul would have wanted to make inroads close to the emperor, he probably would have never been allowed to contact anyone connected with the imperial establishment. But now, in the outworking of the sovereignty of God, circumstances had brought Paul to the capital of the great Roman Empire, where he won converts for Christ among those associated with the emperor! From these important contacts for Christ, the gospel would be spread throughout the Roman Empire as those of Caesar's household shared their faith in Christ with those who had business in the Roman capital.

Paul concluded his letter much as the same as he began it:

The grace of the Lord Jesus Christ be with your spirit (4:23).

To Paul, the word "grace" (*charis*) was more than a salutation (1:2) and complimentary close (4:23) of a letter. This one word reminded Paul that he was deserving of eternal condemnation but that God had sent His only Son to pay the penalty for his sin. Paul had trusted in Christ as his personal Savior and had received forgiveness of sin and eternal life. This marvelous grace of God motivated Paul to do all he did in taking the gospel to a confused, Christ-hating world. Paul's service of love had brought him much suffering, but God had worked through him to accomplish many victories, such as the salvation of the Philippians and those of Caesar's household.

The same grace of God is available to each person today. And like Paul, anyone who places his trust in Christ as his personal Savior from sin receives forgiveness of sin and eternal life. Salvation involves a transfer of trust—from oneself and what he can do to Jesus Christ and what He has done for him.

Have you trusted Christ as your personal Savior? If not, do so before it is eternally too late. Then you will be able to apply Paul's words to yourself: "The grace of the Lord Jesus Christ be with your spirit" (4:23).

Acknowledgments

Authors are pleased when they learn others have benefitted from their writings. When this book was previously published by Back to the Bible, this letter was received from a pastor.

When preaching Philippians, I relied on your commentary on the book. You are the master of word studies that lead to clear application. I have been enriched by your work— God knows how grateful I am.

Pastor David Wiersbe
Caledonia, Minnesota

About the Author

Dr. Harold J. Berry is a former professor of Bible and Greek at Grace University of Omaha. He served for many years as personal assistant to Theodore H. Epp, founder of Back to the Bible. Dr. Berry holds a Master of Theology degree from Dallas Theological Seminary and a Doctor of Divinity from Grace University.